PRAISE FOR *THE 7 PITFALLS OF SINGLE PARENTING*

"Life and love can take unexpected turns, and *The 7 Pitfalls of Single Parenting* offers hope and clear guidance for its readers. Building authentic, loving relationships is the greatest gift we can give our children, and this important book shows you just how to do that."

Barbara De Angelis, PhD., #1 *New York Times* Best-Selling Author, *How Did I Get Here? Finding Your Way to Renewed Hope and Happiness When Life and Love take Unexpected Turns*

"This book will help you discover what kind of life you deeply desire to lead, use the experience of single parenting as a catalyst to get there, and avoid the pi at are bound to arise along the way."

Debl *York Times* Best-Selling Author, *Dark Side of* *Light Chasers*, www.DebbieFord.com

"To go t ok is like adding years of difficult offers the shortest path to g ble resource that I ca

w Firm
k Radio

"This b nts preserve th a good road m; s well as warning tten in a down-t *tfalls* is a resource

hepherd
Co e and e.com *Guide*

"I lo ivorce need .com mon I can see in come wiser

e, LLB ly Law Au th ed)

"*The 7 Pitfalls of Single Parenting* is packed with great insights, clear concepts and helpful activities that make it so easy to implement change in your family right away. As a parent educator for almost 20 years, I've seen firsthand how parents can struggle, and how their children end up paying the price. I now have a book I can highly recommend!"

Beverley Cathcart-Ross,
Founder of the Parenting Network

"This book is a powerful, practical tool for all parents who are considering divorce, going through a divorce, or who are already divorced. I intend to recommend it to all of my mediation clients as an essential step in the healing process necessary to effective co-parenting. The sooner divorcing parents read this book, the easier the transition will be for their children."

Cynthia Tiano, Esquire
Supreme Court Certified Family Mediator and
25-year Divorce Attorney
Author, *Mediate This*! blog, www.MediateThis.com

"For many children, the divorce of their parents is an emotionally devastating milestone that shapes the rest of their lives. Carolyn Ellis brilliantly demystifies how to be a great single parent in this incredible book! I only wish it was available 30 years ago when my own parents divorced."

Alex Mandossian
Founder of Heritage House Publishing, Inc.
www.AlexMandossian.com

"A single parent herself, Carolyn Ellis' love for her children, and for all children living through divorce, comes through loud and clear. With compassion and firmness, she helps parents chart their own path through divorce and its aftermath in a way that can actually benefit their children. *The 7 Pitfalls of Single Parenting* is a much needed guide for parents going through one of the most difficult times they will ever know."

Sandra Demson, LLB
Collaborative Family Lawyer

"Parent-child relationships are so critical for determining the kind of adult your child will grow up to be, so I see this book as a "must-read" for all single parents. Written with compassion, humor, and honesty, this book offers basic principles for effective single parenting that are simple, universal, and will support your child after divorce."

Ken Donaldson, M.A., L.M.H.C.
The REALationship Coach and Author of *Marry YourSelf First!*
Saying "I Do" to a Life of Passion, Power and Purpose

"This practical, fast-moving book gives you a step-by-step plan you can use immediately to achieve greater success in raising your kids after the shock of divorce. If you find life after divorce difficult and want to be able to raise healthy and happy kids, you should absolutely read this book. *The 7 Pitfalls of Single Parenting* will give you a simple and sensible process to help you create joyful relationships with your kids and with yourself. Bottom line: It's simple when you know what to avoid and how to deal with things."

Vered Neta, Trainer, Co-Author, *The Art of Lovemaking: Couples'*
Guide to a Passionate Sex Life

"Carolyn Ellis is giving single parents a great resource. They will find comfort in knowing they are not alone, and that it can and will be different! With examples, exercises and insights, Ellis provides a clear path forward in *The 7 Pitfalls of Single Parenting*. Parents can use this excellent resource to lift themselves up and out of the 7 pitfalls in a structured way and find happiness within themselves, as much as with their kids."

Wouter van der Hall
Author of The Parent Program™

"As a child of divorce myself, I so wish that my parents had been able to read this book! It gives you clear strategies so you can avoid the minefields and heal your family."

Sandy Grason, Author of *Journalution: Journaling to Awaken Your*
Inner Voice, Heal Your Life and Manifest Your Dreams

"As the partner of a divorced man, this book helped me to be more supportive to him, as he navigates the often murky waters with his ex. I recommend this book to anyone who is even remotely connected to someone going through a divorce that involves children."

Coco Fossland, Founder, WorldChangingBusiness

THE 7 PITFALLS OF SINGLE PARENTING

THE 7 PITFALLS OF SINGLE PARENTING

WHAT TO AVOID TO HELP YOUR CHILDREN THRIVE AFTER DIVORCE

CAROLYN B. ELLIS

iUniverse, Inc.
New York Lincoln Shanghai

THE 7 PITFALLS OF SINGLE PARENTING
What to Avoid to Help Your Children Thrive After Divorce

iUniverse books may be ordered through booksellers or by contacting:

iUniverse
1663 Liberty Drive
Bloomington, IN 47403
www.iuniverse.com
1-800-Authors (1-800-288-4677)

Because of the dynamic nature of the Internet, any Web addresses or links contained in this book may have changed since publication and may no longer be valid.

This publication is designed to educate and provide general information regarding the subject matter covered. The reader is encouraged to consult with his or her own advisors regarding specific situations. The views expressed in this work are solely those of the author and do not necessarily reflect the views of the publisher, and the publisher hereby disclaims any responsibility for them.

Many names and identifying details of the individual examples described in this book have been changed to preserve confidentiality.

ISBN: 978-1-936236-94-7 (sc)
ISBN: 978-1-936236-95-4 (e)

Library of Congress Control Number: 2011961817

Printed in the United States of America

iUniverse rev. date: 02/20/2012

To my life's greatest teachers:

Erin, Kyle, and Matthew.

Thank you for the inspiration and the joy I experience with you each day!

CONTENTS

PART ONE
SO NOW YOU'RE A SINGLE PARENT

PART TWO
ESTABLISH A STRONG FOUNDATION

PART THREE
THE 7 PITFALLS

PART FOUR
THRIVE AFTER DIVORCE

ACKNOWLEDGEMENTS

It's been an incredible journey to birth a book and there have been so many supporters cheering me along the way. I am deeply grateful to them for their encouragement and for sharing my vision that one can indeed thrive after divorce.

First, to the many individuals who shared their own experience of divorce with me as clients, teleclass students, interview subjects, individuals, and divorce buddies, I thank you. I appreciate your trust and honesty. By sharing your heartaches and triumphs, you shine a path in the darkness for other people.

To Barbara De Angelis, thank you for your enduring love, profound support and fierce commitment to my freedom. In every moment you are a model of wisdom, love, integrity and expansion. I am truly blessed and honored to be a part of the cosmic advance team you have created.

To Debbie Ford, words cannot express the incredible gratitude I feel for your role and guidance in showing me how to truly turn my divorce into a catalyst for an extraordinary life. I will always hold a special place in my heart for you and the beautiful integrative coaching community you have birthed.

I couldn't have done this without the support of my incredible believing mirrors: Diann Craven, Susan Glavin, Kathleen Griffiths, Donna Karson, Petra Lackey and Danielle Merrill. I treasure the wisdom, connection and support we share and consider you as sisters.

Special thanks to Anne Fenn, my original divorce buddy, for teaching me that my feelings mattered. To Jeff Malone, a rock of support whose unconditional support has allowed me to spread my wings. To Diana Shepherd, thank you for your friendship and stalwart support.

To my former husband, I thank you for being such an important part of my life and for the gift of our three children. I appreciate what a wonderful and dedicated dad you are to them.

I'd like to thank my parents, Jack and Barbara Ellis, for always believing and trusting in me. I feel your love and unconditional support daily. Thanks to my sister, Andrea, for being in my corner.

Heartfelt thanks to my soul sister, Susan Glavin. Thank you for always seeing that bigger vision so clearly and lovingly holding me to it. Words can't express the depth of appreciation I feel for having you as my buddy.

Finally, I would like to thank my amazing children! To Erin, thank you for telling it straight and playing full out. To Kyle, thank you for your gentleness and amazing laugh. To Matthew, thank you for your thought-provoking questions and being my volleyball partner. I know there have been many times when Mom has disappeared in front of her computer or has been traveling, and I appreciate your patience and loving support of me. You are three of the wisest, most honest and loving human beings I know. I am blessed to be your mother.

FOREWORD

In my own career as an author, speaker and transformational teacher, I have helped millions of people transform themselves, their relationships, and their lives. And believe it or not, one of the most transformational experiences anyone can go through is the process of divorce. No one who has ever taken this journey forgets the moment when you finally admit to yourself that the relationship you're in isn't working, and that it's time to leave. You wish you could go to sleep, wake up the next morning and have everything be different, but you can't. You wish your partner would magically become the person you want him or her to be, that that isn't going to happen. Whether you or your partner initiated the decision to end the relationship, the pain of saying good-bye still feels like it is too much to bear.

This excruciating and difficult decision is made even worse, of course, when you have children. No parent wants to be a source of unhappiness to their children, whom they love more than life itself, and therefore the guilt that accompanies breaking up can be devastating. And as if this weren't enough, you suddenly find yourself navigating the frightening waters of single parenthood.

When my own parents divorced in 1963, I was eleven years old. I know that both of them, especially my beloved mother, found themselves frightened, lost, and in pain. At the time, not only was divorce a terrible stigma, but there was virtually no help or support of any kind to guide divorced parents through the complicated and emotionally treacherous minefield of bringing up children post-divorce. Even now, it is bittersweet for me to think of how much my mother would have treasured this book you have been wise enough to purchase, to know she was not alone in the turbulent ocean of her emotions, to know her questions were normal, and most of all, to have someone as her guide who could offer her wise, compassionate and practical answers that would provide her with the courage and clarity she needed as a single parent.

Fortunately for you, the wisdom and guidance my mother and so many millions of other divorced parents had to do with *has* been beautifully articulated in Carolyn Ellis' important and invaluable book. *The 7 Pitfalls of Single Parenting* will help you recognize and understand the road from divorce to recovery, along with all its roadblocks and detours, so that you can move through them and around them with less fear, confusion and guilt, and more grace, dignity, and harmony.

This book is truly an offering of love and service from a wonderful coach, teacher, and most of all, successful single parent who has used her own journey to transform and expand not only herself and her bond with her children, but also to create smart, effective strategies that have helped tens of thousands of divorced single parents just like you. By deciding to read this book, you have already taken an important step on the road to rebuilding your life, your family and most of all, your relationship with love. And your commitment to learn how to go through this time in your life in the most conscious way possible is the best gift you could give yourself, your children…and yes, even your ex.

I promise you that the very thing you may believe was a painful dead end is about to become a powerful doorway, leading you to a new, deeply fulfilling and joyful life that is just waiting to be discovered.

Offered in love,
Barbara De Angelis Ph.D.
#1 *New York Times* Best-Selling Author
"How Did I Get Here?"
"Are You The One For Me?"
"Real Moments"
"Secrets About Men Every Woman Should Know"

PREFACE

Separation and divorce for families can be brutal. This is especially so when children are caught in the crossfire between parents who are hurt, angry, misinformed, and often seriously misguided in what they think is best for their children. The expense of starting over is complicated by the need to try to run two separated homes on an income that could barely support one unified household. Lawyers' fees, while sometimes unavoidable, often only make matters worse. Emotions are drained. The stress often makes couples ill. Divorce is depressing and lonely. Sounds bleak, doesn't it? It is, and that is why books like this one by Carolyn Ellis are so important, as guides for parents who face the prospect of single parenting.

Carolyn Ellis has taken her considerable education and common sense, combined it with her divorce and parenting experience, and managed to distill some helpful wisdom that can save other parents stress, expense, and wasted time. There are pitfalls in being a single parent post-separation and post-divorce some obvious and some not so obvious. Carolyn has provided not only clear warning signs for these pitfalls, but also a common sense map for avoiding them altogether.

Her approach provides an important contribution to thinking and planning for a post-separation and post-divorce life that will be good not only for the parent, but peaceful and safe for the children as well.

Her recommended strategies call for parents to work on behalf of themselves and their children, but that work will pay huge dividends.

MICHAEL G. COCHRANE, BA, LLB

INTRODUCTION

"The greater danger for most of us is not that our aim is too high and we miss it, but that it is too low and we reach it."

Michelangelo

If you're reading this book, you may already be divorced or separated, or perhaps you're thinking about it.

I know how much of a roller-coaster ride divorce can be from my own experience. I found my divorce process to be devastating, confusing, inspiring, challenging, liberating, and disorienting all at the same time. To help you understand where I'm coming from and how this book came to life as a result, I'd like to share some of my own story with you.

I appeared to "have it all": an Ivy-league education, a successful career, a happy marriage to my high school sweetheart, and three healthy children. When I started my family more than twenty years ago, I had dreams of living happily ever after. My children would grow up and start happy families of their own. My husband and I would grow old together, reminiscing in our rocking chairs about what a beautiful life's journey we had shared. Did you have a fairy tale dream like this too?

One night, my husband and I went to a great romantic movie and had dinner together. Over appetizers, he told me he felt our marriage was in trouble. We didn't have that passionate "zing" he wanted in a relationship. In that moment, I felt like time had stopped.

On a certain level, this was all news to me! My chest felt like it was caught in a vise. My palms went clammy, and I could hardly breathe. As I watched my tears fall into my soup at the restaurant, I felt all of my dreams and aspirations for my "happily ever after" fairy tale come crashing down.

Yet at another level, this conversation confirmed something that my gut had been telling me for quite a long time. We had become different people than we were twenty years earlier. We had grown apart; we took each other for granted. We weren't making our marriage a priority. In my heart of hearts, I wasn't sure I had what it would take to put Humpty Dumpty (our marriage) back together again. In retrospect, I appreciate the courage it took for my husband to tell me the truth.

In the months following that memorable dinner date, I was determined to leave no stone unturned in either repairing the relationship or ending it gracefully. I threw myself into every possible therapy, marriage counseling, relationship workshop, and self-help program to try to "figure it out." I could have opened a small independent bookstore with the mountain of books I devoured on divorce, parenting, psychology, personal development, and self-help. Yet after two years of trying to put the marriage back together again, I realized I wanted a divorce.

My Turning Point

A major turning point for me came one day in an interaction I had with my children. My son, who was about seven at the time, came out of his room one morning to ask me a question. In that moment, I snapped at him. I don't know what it was, but I bellowed at him and then doubled over and screamed in frustration and anger. Have you ever had a moment when you've totally lost it and dumped your toxic emotions onto your child?

After my emotional meltdown, I stood up and looked at my young son who was still standing in front of me. Something about the way he looked at me in that moment changed my life. In his eyes, I saw that something had broken inside of him, some piece of his little heart, and that I had done that. He handled it quite gracefully and said to me, "Oh boy, I think I better go back to my room now," and turned on his heel and went back to his room.

That was the kick in the pants I needed to take action and take responsibility for what I was creating in my life. I was responsible for whether I'd raise my three children in an atmosphere that was loving and harmonious, or toxic and embittered. So in that moment, I decided that I would do *whatever* it took to heal my own heart and wounds so I could give my children all the love, encouragement, and support they deserved. I realized I had a profound choice to make: I could either lick my wounds for another twenty years, or I could take my pain and use it to heal myself and others. At the time of my separation, my children were only nine, seven, and three.

A New Journey Begins

It is said that when the student is ready, the teacher appears. The week I decided to end our marriage in 2001, I stumbled across a very powerful book that changed my life. It is *Spiritual Divorce: Divorce as a Catalyst for an Extraordinary Life* by *New York Times* best-selling author Debbie Ford. I highly recommend that you read it. Ford outlines seven spiritual laws of divorce that can help anyone who's ever been wounded from a relationship to heal their heart. (For other resources, please see the "Recommended Resources" section at the end of this book.)

The message and tools in *Spiritual Divorce* were so illuminating for me that I decided in 2002 to train as an integrative coach with Debbie Ford's Institute for Integrative Coaching. Since then, I've taken every training program on coaching the Institute has offered, including specialized training in divorce coaching based on a curriculum from *Spiritual Divorce*. I left a successful career in fundraising to pursue my vision of being a coach and author. I have served as a staff coach for the Institute, which is now a part of John F. Kennedy University in California, and is the first training program for coaching to become part of an accredited university. I'm honored to have helped train hundreds of people to become coaches. Over the past five years, I have had the privilege of working with individual clients and leading teleclasses with participants from all over the world.

What has been the impact of this work on my own family? I've seen true miracles take place in my relationship with my children. The light in my heart for my children outshines any of the accomplishments I've experienced in the professional arena. I feel blessed and inspired by my three children on a daily basis now, and I am able to be present with them. I learn so much by being their mom, and I think my children are my greatest teachers! I always had what I considered to be a great relationship with my kids. Now the relationship I have with my children is truly extraordinary—the love, connection, and support we have for each other is far deeper than I ever imagined it could be.

Seeing my children and me thrive after divorce filled me with such inspiration, joy, and passion that I decided to create Thrive After Divorce Inc. My company is dedicated to empowering separated and divorced individuals who can fearlessly create and express their highest potential. It offers a variety of educational resources (books, e-books, audio products, and e-courses) and live training (teleseminars and workshops). Through Thrive After Divorce, I hope to share the insights and tools I've discovered to support thousands of separated and divorced individuals and families around the globe. This book is the first step in that process.

You Are Not Alone

Divorce is widespread in today's society. If you're not divorced or separated, you most likely know someone who has experienced it, or you have experienced it yourself as a child of divorce. Divorce is a growing reality for more and more parents and children around the globe.

Here are some of the latest facts about divorce in North America:

- The Institute for Divorce Financial Analysts (IDFA) estimated in 2005 that more than 33 million people in North America were divorced and another 5 million were separated.[1]
- Demographers estimate between 40–60 percent of all current marriages will end in divorce.[2]
- New divorces will involve more than one million children in the United States and more than 36,000 children in Canada annually.[3]
- The number of children living in a single parent family has doubled since 1970. Based on current trends, it is predicted that upwards of 70 percent of children born since 1980 will spend some time living in a single-parent home before their eighteenth birthday.[4]
- The IDFA estimates that approximately $50 billion is spent annually in North America as a direct result of divorce, with one-third of that going toward legal fees.[5]

The Impact of Divorce on Children

Divorce is a major life transition. Its impact cuts across many significant areas of life: financial, social, emotional, economical, occupational, geographical, and spiritual. Children are inevitably affected when their family separates into two households. Separation and divorce are not legacies that need to be passed on from one generation to the next.

Researchers have done a multitude of longitudinal studies comparing children whose parents are divorced with children of married parents. According to researcher Dr. Joan Kelly, who gave a public presentation on children's adjustment to divorce based on her 30 years of research and work in the field, there is a higher risk of problems for divorced children, and children's degree of resiliency in adjusting to the changes and stresses caused by divorce is of paramount concern.[6]

External social problems, which were found consistently through numerous research studies, can include:

- Aggressive, impulsive, and anti-social behavior
- Relationship problems with peers, authority figures, and parents
- Academic and achievement problems, with children of divorce two to three times more likely to drop out of school
- Twice as many teenage births

Research also found internal emotional issues are triggered for children of divorce, such as anxiety, depression, and lower self-esteem. Dr. Kelly's research showed that 20% of the symptoms exhibited by divorced children could be accounted for by the pre-divorce situation and children growing up in a stressful, unhappily married family.

These are sobering facts, but need to be put in the context that research studies do find a large degree of overlap between children from divorced families and married families. The majority of divorced children function within an average range on standardized tests. Dr. Kelly noted that between 75-80% function well within normal psychological, behavioral, and social parameters. Competent and caring parenting is critical in determining the impact of divorce on children.

Get Yourself a Road Map

Assuming you are a parent who is divorced, separated, or headed in that direction, would you be interested in having a road map to guide you in your future?

Perhaps you have made a mistake in your life and then looked back on it and thought, "I wish someone had warned me about that ahead of time!"

Would you like to make sure that your children thrive after your divorce and blossom into emotionally well-adjusted, loving, and responsible individuals who can fearlessly create and express their highest potential?

If you answered YES to any of these questions, you're in the right place at the right time with the right tool in your hand. I believe divorce shouldn't be something you need to "survive" or "get through." Of course, divorced people face tough challenges, but they face great opportunities as well. If you intend to thrive and flourish after divorce, you will. This book will give you insights and tools to make that intention a reality.

Henry Ford once said, "Whether you think you can or you think you can't, you're right." What you experience as a result of your divorce will be affected significantly by your mind-set and intention as you embark on this journey.

It takes a lot of courage and faith to create a union and bring children into the world. It takes just as much courage and faith to end your relationship in such a way that you and your children are healthy, intact, and willing to create a future that excites you. Reading this book and acting upon it is a great first step.

Why Does the World Need Another Divorce Book?

Where I am today is a result of me becoming aware of the pitfalls described in this book and navigating my way through them. Believe me, I have made all of these mistakes myself! This is the book I wish had existed when I was starting out as a single parent.

I used to get frustrated with all the information out there and the process of sorting out what was relevant to me. I'd find a great strategy in chapter seven of one parenting book and then a useful insight in another divorce book. I had to connect the dots to make these random pieces of information useful, relevant, and practical to my job as a mom of three young children.

My frustration that the one comprehensive book I was seeking didn't exist led me to write this book. My hope is that this book will prevent other single parents from having to reinvent the wheel and will help them be better prepared as parents. Having a "user's guide" like this would have saved me countless hours of heartache, confusion, self-doubt, and conflict.

To write this book, I immersed myself in research. I interviewed experts on relationships, parenting, and divorce. I also interviewed and spoke with dozens of single parents, and I am very grateful for their sharing. In 2006, I led a number of teleseminars with single parents where I further "road tested" many of the concepts and solutions presented here. I thank the dozens of single parents from all over North America who provided their feedback and insights to my research as I developed this book. Throughout the book I have used real-life examples from my clients, students, and interviews. The anecdotes offered in the book are based on real people—only the names have been changed.

Yes, divorce leaves an indelible mark on your heart and your life. Unfortunately many people remain perpetual victims of their divorce. Their parenting skills are colored by those festering wounds as a result of that choice.

But divorce also brings with it possibilities that would never have been available otherwise. I set an intention to thrive after divorce and not to settle for simply surviving or "getting through" this life-altering experience.

I invite you to join me in choosing to thrive after divorce. You, too, can make the powerful choice that somehow, some way, you can let this profound experience be something that you can use for your own well-being. You can choose to not remain stuck and embittered because of your failed relationship. I invite you to choose to thrive after divorce, not only for your own sake, but for the sake of your children.

How to Use This Book

In this book, I've identified what I consider to be the seven most common pitfalls that single parents can experience and how to avoid them. Awareness is the first step to successfully navigating the waters of being a single parent. The purpose of this book is to show you that even though you are facing the challenges of raising children as a single parent, you can create a situation where you and your children don't merely "survive" a divorce. Instead, you and your children can come through divorce in a way that you all thrive!

The journey of a thousand miles begins with a single step, so acknowledge yourself right now for taking the time to find and obtain this book! After much research, observation, and my personal experience over the last six years of raising my three children as a single parent, I believe there are seven major categories of mistakes, or pitfalls. They are:

1.   Not having the big picture
2.   Getting hooked by your ex-spouse
3.   Parenting from guilt
4.   Going for the martyr medal
5.   Not putting the kids first
6.   Being responsible for your children's relationship with your ex
7.   Living in chaos

If you find yourself the subject of any kind of physical abuse or violent behavior, or if you feel that you or your children are being in threatened in any way, you should seek professional help immediately. The strategies and guidance for parenting here may not always be appropriate in cases where domestic violence or threats to physical safety exist. If you feel you are at risk of any danger, please contact the police, your physician, or another professional service provider.

Chapter Overview

A chapter is devoted to each pitfall. Each chapter includes:

- A definition of the pitfall, including signs you may be stuck
- The costs of being in the pitfall and the impact it may have on your parenting skills
- Strategies and perspectives to help you disengage from the pitfall
- Action steps listing questions and practical steps you can take today to break free of negative, single-parenting pitfalls and help your children thrive after divorce. These action steps are meant to get you moving in simple ways to incorporate the information into your life.

Accountability Check

At the end of each action step, you'll find an Accountability Check that looks like this:

✔ Accountability Check

☐   I will complete this exercise by: _____

☐   I completed this exercise on: _____

♪ *Remember to Celebrate!* ♪

Write down the date you plan to complete the exercise. A written commitment is far more powerful and binding than one you make to yourself in your head. After you've completed the exercise, write the completion date down as well.

As a single parent myself, I appreciate how busy and demanding your schedule is. I've designed this book to give you the best information available and deliver it in an effective and time-efficient way so you can incorporate these tools immediately into your parenting. Instead of only arming you with knowledge, I want to help you put this information to work right away in your role as a parent. I encourage you to take the time to complete the action steps—after all, we learn by doing!

"Take Action!" Tracker

At the end of the book is the "Take Action!" Tracker, which allows you to see all of the exercises contained in the book in one place so you can easily check off the ones you've done. It's a great way to get a sense of your progress and the actions you'll take as a result of working with the material in this book. There will be a reminder at the end of each chapter to log your activity in the "Take Action!" Tracker.

If you want to work at a deeper and more comprehensive level, you can order the *The 7 Pitfalls of Single Parenting Workbook*. This workbook contains more exercises, specific worksheets, and checklists, and is designed to complement the information in this book. Visit www.7pitfalls.com for more information.

The Importance of Celebrating Your Success

You can use the Accountability Checks and the "Take Action!" Tracker to measure your progress and gain a sense of satisfaction that you are taking concrete action toward improving your parenting skills. When you complete each exercise, take a moment to celebrate your accomplishment. You can do a victory dance, give yourself a pat on the back, or do whatever it takes to mark your accomplishment in some kind of physical way. If it makes you feel silly, that's great—do it!

Take a moment right now to tune into what the little voice in your head is telling you at the thought of you doing a victory dance after you finish an exercise in this book. What is it saying? "Oh come on, I'm a grown-up and I don't need to do that stuff!" or "That is just plain silly! I'll do the exercise, but I won't pat myself on the back."

If your inner voice is saying anything along those lines, you've just learned an important lesson about how you live your life. As one of my mentors, T. Harv Eker, says, "How you do anything is how you do everything." If that kind of resistance or internal bargaining is showing up here, it is undoubtedly showing up in other places in your life. Do you stop and acknowledge yourself when you have a great moment with your children? Or are you so busy moving on to the next item on your "to do" list that you don't pause to "smell the roses?"

The important habit we all need to cultivate is to celebrate our successes. So if celebrating your success feels uncomfortable or awkward to you, that's fine, but just try it anyway. To paraphrase Albert Einstein, the definition of insanity is doing the same thing over and over again and expecting different results. You got this book to learn something new, and this is a big lesson right here!

If you're still reluctant to celebrate your successes, just think of the example you want to set for your children. Do you want your children to create a life-long habit of ignoring or minimizing their accomplishments? My invitation to you is to simply try on a new behavior. If you don't like it after you've finished working with the material in this book, you can go back to your old patterns again! I promise.

PART ONE

SO NOW YOU'RE
A SINGLE PARENT

CHAPTER ONE

The Challenges of Being a Single Parent

"A woman is like a tea bag.
You never know how strong she is
until she gets into hot water."

Eleanor Roosevelt

Definition of a Single Parent

The term "single parent" commonly describes an individual who has at least one child and is the only adult in the household. Another term that is growing in usage is "co-parent." There are actually a few different types of single parents:

- The parent who is separated or divorced, and the other parent takes an active coparenting role
- The parent who is separated or divorced, and the other parent, for whatever reason, does not take an active role in parenting the children or even have contact with them

- The parent who is single because of the death of a spouse
- The parent who is single by choice, such as by use of a donor sperm bank, and the biological parent has never been involved with the child.

The primary audience for whom this book was written is the first two groups: single parents where the other parent is still alive and may or may not have a role in coparenting the children. However, many of the pitfalls described in this book are equally applicable to all parents, whether single, married, or widowed.

This book will generally use the term "ex-spouse" to identify the other parent of your children. Some relationships are sanctified by marriage, so your "ex" was indeed a "spouse." Some may not involve marriage, so the term "partner" may be more accurate. For the purposes of simplicity, I will use the term "ex-spouse" to make it clear we are talking about the person with whom you had children. As a further note, the information in this book is equally applicable to same-sex and heterosexual partners.

Your Journey Will Be Unique to You

Everyone's journey is unique, so there is no one-size-fits-all formula for mitigating the impact divorce can have on our children. However, single parents generally face some very common pitfalls that can damage their children in the long run. The dictionary defines "pitfall" as "an unapparent source of trouble or danger, a hidden hazard" and as "an unconcealed hole in the ground, a trap." There can be many ways that single parents can, either through the best of intentions or simply from ignorance or inexperience, unwittingly harm their children's emotional transition through the separation and divorce process.

Parenting is one of the most demanding jobs on the planet at the best of times, but to parent a child when your own heart is wounded from your relationship breakdown just adds to its complexity and challenge. Experts agree two factors play a key role in children's well-being after divorce. The first factor is maintaining family relationships that existed prior to the divorce. Children benefit from maintaining familial relations in their life that were important and meaningful to them prior to the divorce, says Constance Ahrons, author of *The Good Divorce*. The second factor is a "generally supportive and cooperative" relationship between the parents, whether married or divorced. These two factors are "the foundation for a child's true best interests," asserts Ahrons, and "differentiates between the children who are and are not damaged by divorce."[7]

At one point, we loved our partners deeply, felt an intimate emotional connection with them, started a family with them, and dreamed of living "happily ever after" with them. With a divorce, that dream dies. Experts say it can take you at least a year to get past the initial painful and negative stages of divorce. Some people may take between three to five years to process the emotional fallout from separation.[8] What I've found, however, is you can create a new and powerful dream for yourself as a single parent out of the ashes of your broken relationship if you're willing to learn the lessons available.

The Phases of Separating Emotionally

Psychology has many models of how human beings grieve a loss, whether it's the loss of a loved one through death or divorce.[9] The model below is a simple one that summarizes the major stages.

Recovering from divorce is very similar to the grieving process we experience when a loved one dies. We lose an important part of our life. The divorce process has five stages, which are very similar to the stages people experience in grief. The stages are not necessarily experienced in this order, and people may re-cycle through the stages during their separation process:

- **Shock:** Whether you initiated the divorce or not, you will be in shock. Your social identity, your economic situation, and your relationship with family and friends all undergo a major readjustment. When you're in shock, a part of you shuts down and goes into autopilot as a defense from the emotional trauma. You may feel numb or disconnected from your feelings. The shock state is fueled by the fear of "what's next"—fear fueled by the realization that your old life is ending. This is the stage where literally all you can do is take it one day at a time.

- **Anger:** In this stage, you connect with your feelings, the ones that are right at the surface—anger, blame, resentment, and anxiety. Like a wounded animal, you lash out in pain against the perpetrator. This is the phase where gossip and blame kick into high gear. In the anger phase, you feel like the victim, and everything is being done *to* you. You enlist others around you into a story of powerlessness because it's a way to feel support. Blaming others for your misery and receiving sympathy offers a temporary feeling of power. You're in a reactive mode and generally not willing to be self-reflective. In the anger phase, you can't see any lesson from the pain of your relationship. In fact, you're not even open to looking for the lessons.

- **Transition:** In this phase, the emotional roller coaster really starts to take off. You feel conflicting emotions from one moment to the next. You're sad and full of regret one minute. Then you're hopeful and positive about being a single parent the next. You have some sense of yourself as an individual again, not just being identified as "one half" of a couple. In the transition phase, you are more willing to look at your own role in the relationship breakdown and to seek out the wisdom from this crisis.

- **Grief:** In this phase, you feel consumed by sadness and loneliness. You feel the loss of having an intimate partner to share your life. Even if ending the marriage was your choice and you don't want to be with that person anymore, you will likely still experience the grief phase. This is the time when you mourn your losses—of your partner, of your vision of you as part of a happily married couple, of your children's lives under the same roof with their parents, and of your change in your social network.

- **Acceptance:** You can now accept the old relationship is over. You're putting the framework for a working partnership with your ex-spouse in place. You feel like you're moving forward toward a new life. You accept that everything happens for a reason. You are creating a vision of a new future for yourself and your children, which magnetically pulls you forward, out of the heartbreak from the past.

Emotionally digesting your divorce is NOT a linear process. You'll likely cycle through these various phases. Trigger events or relationship milestones may plunge you back into one of these phases. Examples of trigger events would include your wedding anniversary, seeing your ex with a new partner, or seeing a photograph of you in happier times. Hearing your children talk about their other parent's new relationship and the inevitability of traditional celebrations, like Valentine's Day or Christmas, will test you regularly. Over time, your ability to move through to acceptance and the length of time you feel "stuck" in any of the other phases will change.

If you've just recently separated and believe that you're emotionally over the separation or divorce within a short period of time, take a moment to get really honest with yourself. You may simply be "managing" your feelings. It's important that you allow yourself time for your healing to take place. If you rush that process, you will inevitably bring those old emotional wounds into your future relationships. The prospect of repeating heartache and disappointment with future romantic partners was a great motivator for me to take the time I needed to heal emotionally.

Children Go Through a Separation Process Too

Quite often, when you parent from a tender and wounded emotional state, you lose your balance and emotional control. Despite your best intentions, you end up wounding the innocent bystanders of your divorce—your children. This book was written so you can bypass some of the most common, single-parenting pitfalls. This book will give you more empowering habits and beliefs for your parenting toolkit. Just as adults must go through a process to cope with the emotional impact of separation, children must as well.

Children go through similar emotional phases that adults do, but there are some important factors to consider:

- **"It's My Fault"**: Children use a filter of "what this means about me" in interpreting events in their world. In their early stages of emotional development, children are instinctively self-referential. Children conclude that if something happens, like a divorce, it must be because they "did something wrong." Children often believe they are the reason Mommy and Daddy are splitting up.

   It's very important, therefore, when you explain your separation to your child that you make it clear that divorce is the result of issues between two grown-ups. Children aren't the cause.

- **The Reunion Fantasy**: Children often fantasize that Mommy and Daddy can and should get back together again. Even though we live in a day and age where divorce is more common than ever, children yearn for their parents to reunite. The desire for parents to be together can often be held even when children become adults themselves. Often children believe that if they are "really good" children or negotiate and bargain with their parents, they may be able to get their parents to reconcile.

   I believe part of this fantasy comes from children wanting to be loved. It's hard to understand they are truly loved by both parents if both parents live separately under two roofs. It's important to reassure your child that they are loved no matter what by both mom and dad, even if mom and dad no longer love each other.

- **A Chip Off the Old Block**: Children see themselves as the product of a mom and a dad. When their parents split up, their self-esteem is thrown into question. "If Daddy doesn't love Mommy anymore, and half of me comes from Mommy, does that mean there's something Daddy can't love about me too?" A child's awareness of being the product of two parents is one reason why it's never advisable to bad-mouth, malign, or openly criticize the other parent to the child.

CHAPTER TWO

Where Are You Right Now?

---

*"Live as if you were to die tomorrow.
Learn as if you were to live forever. "*

Mahatma Ghandi

Before you dig into this book, it's important and very useful to get a picture of where you are right now with your single-parenting skills. The self-assessment quiz in this chapter is designed to measure your current attitudes, actions, and beliefs that relate specifically to the seven pitfalls of single parenting. This will give you a baseline of where you are and tell you whether you're already stuck in some patterns that will leave you feeling powerless. The quiz will only take you a few moments to complete.

You can fill out the self-assessment test manually in this book, or if you prefer, you can complete it online and have the results tabulated instantly and sent to your e-mail address. To complete it online, simply visit www.7pitfalls.com.

After you've completed the book and followed the recommended action plans, take the self-assessment quiz again in ninety days. See what's changed in terms of your results. You will be pleasantly surprised!

7 Pitfalls of Single Parenting Self-Assessment Quiz

For each question, rank yourself on a scale of 1–5 as to your level of agreement with the statement (1 represents strongly disagree and 5 represents strongly agree). Go with your initial gut response to the statement and complete the quiz as quickly as you can.

7 PITFALLS OF SINGLE PARENTING: QUIZ

1. I feel my divorce will damage my children emotionally for life.
   1 ☐   2 ☐   3 ☐   4 ☐   5 ☐

2. Most of my friends are happily married and are raising their children together under one roof.
   1 ☐   2 ☐   3 ☐   4 ☐   5 ☐

3. When people ask if I'm married, I feel a twinge of guilt and shame when I say I'm divorced.
   1 ☐   2 ☐   3 ☐   4 ☐   5 ☐

4. I notice my children are embarrassed or uncomfortable when they explain to their friends that their parents are divorced.
   1 ☐   2 ☐   3 ☐   4 ☐   5 ☐

5. Because I see my children less now than when I was married, it's even more important that the time we do spend together is positive and upbeat. I make sure my children are doing a lot more activities and having some really fun vacations with me now, even if I can't really afford it.
   1 ☐   2 ☐   3 ☐   4 ☐   5 ☐

6. Life is so busy these days with work, family obligations, and the children's schedule that there's hardly any time to sit down and unwind.
   1 ☐   2 ☐   3 ☐   4 ☐   5 ☐

7. I don't like to ask others for help because it makes me feel weak or needy.
   1 ☐   2 ☐   3 ☐   4 ☐   5 ☐

8. I often wake up tired in the morning.
   1 ☐   2 ☐   3 ☐   4 ☐   5 ☐

9. My kids really need me to be strong so they can get through this divorce intact.
   1 ☐   2 ☐   3 ☐   4 ☐   5 ☐

10. I tend to rush from one appointment to the next because I have so much to do.

1 ☐   2 ☐   3 ☐   4 ☐   5 ☐

11. I don't have time to exercise or take time alone very often.

1 ☐   2 ☐   3 ☐   4 ☐   5 ☐

12. I have to be strong so my children will see that we'll be OK.

1 ☐   2 ☐   3 ☐   4 ☐   5 ☐

13. Despite my best efforts, I often yell at my children over little things.

1 ☐   2 ☐   3 ☐   4 ☐   5 ☐

14. I feel guilty and responsible for depriving my children of having a regular two-parent family to grow up in.

1 ☐   2 ☐   3 ☐   4 ☐   5 ☐

15. I don't like to be a burden to anybody.

1 ☐   2 ☐   3 ☐   4 ☐   5 ☐

16. I am never able to plan more than a few days ahead.

1 ☐   2 ☐   3 ☐   4 ☐   5 ☐

17. I feel overwhelmed by the daily challenges I face and spend a lot of time and energy figuring out what I should do next.

1 ☐   2 ☐   3 ☐   4 ☐   5 ☐

18. I don't like the idea of planning. I feel that it limits my ability to be spontaneous and creative.

1 ☐   2 ☐   3 ☐   4 ☐   5 ☐

19. I dread the thought that I'm going to have to deal with my ex-spouse for the rest of my children's lives.

1 ☐   2 ☐   3 ☐   4 ☐   5 ☐

20. When my ex-spouse does something I don't like, I lose my temper and get upset.

1 ☐   2 ☐   3 ☐   4 ☐   5 ☐

21. I don't know how I'll ever be able to raise my children with my ex. I wish I could just do it on my own and never have to deal with him/her.

1 ☐   2 ☐   3 ☐   4 ☐   5 ☐

22. I worry that my ex will malign or talk badly about me, as a person and as a parent, to family and friends.

1 ☐   2 ☐   3 ☐   4 ☐   5 ☐

23. If I want to do something that I think will hurt someone's feelings, I often use that as a reason not to do it or to do it without them finding out.

1 □   2 □   3 □   4 □   5□

24. It's important to me that people like me and think I'm doing a good job.

1 □   2 □   3 □   4 □   5 □

25. If I ask for something from my ex, I never feel heard. If it's really important, I get my children to make a request on my behalf.

1 □   2 □   3 □   4 □   5 □

26. It's important that my children learn what their father/mother is really like, so I openly share all my feelings about my ex with my children.

1 □   2 □   3 □   4 □   5 □

27. My job is to make sure that my ex-spouse listens to and responds appropriately to my children.

1 □   2 □   3 □   4 □   5 □

28. When my children return from a visit with my ex-spouse, I routinely ask them what they did and how they felt seeing their father/mother.

1 □   2 □   3 □   4 □   5 □

29. My children are too young to communicate effectively to my ex-spouse about what they want or to explain how they feel.

1 □   2 □   3 □   4 □   5 □

30. I get upset when I hear that my ex-spouse has different rules in his/her house about bedtimes/TV watching/discipline.

1 □   2 □   3 □   4 □   5 □

31. If my children are upset by something my ex did, I don't hesitate to pick up the phone and tell him/her off.

1 □   2 □   3 □   4 □   5 □

32. I have trouble pinning down when the children will be at my house or my ex's house, and then putting it on a calendar.

1 □   2 □   3 □   4 □   5 □

33. When my ex or I need to switch our child-sharing arrangements, it always seems to become a battle or big negotiation. We don't have any set rules or agreements about how to handle those requests.

1 □   2 □   3 □   4 □   5 □

34. When there are problems with moving the children or their things between my house and my ex's house, I prefer to solve the problem on my own and then present the answer to my children and my ex-spouse afterward.

   1 ☐   2 ☐   3 ☐   4 ☐   5 ☐

35. I don't like a lot of structure in my household because I prefer to do things on the spur of the moment.

   1 ☐   2 ☐   3 ☐   4 ☐   5 ☐

36. It's my responsibility to make sure my children are happy as much as possible. If they get angry or scared, I feel I'm not doing my job as a parent properly.

   1 ☐   2 ☐   3 ☐   4 ☐   5 ☐

37. I don't enjoy being alone. If I am alone, I prefer to keep my mind occupied with activities such as watching TV, talking to friends, shopping, or doing other activities that keep me busy.

   1 ☐   2 ☐   3 ☐   4 ☐   5 ☐

38. Sometimes I have the same thought patterns about what a jerk my ex-spouse is and how I should have handled things differently. I keep replaying the past in my mind and looking at what I should have done differently.

   1 ☐   2 ☐   3 ☐   4 ☐   5 ☐

39. When I think about my future, I feel sad and disappointed that my dreams of living "happily ever after" never came true. It's hard for me to feel inspired about the future.

   1 ☐   2 ☐   3 ☐   4 ☐   5 ☐

40. Even though we're separated, I think it's important that my ex-spouse and I have the same goals and rules about how to raise our children. The fact that we don't agree about parenting styles is a big source of frustration for me.

   1 ☐   2 ☐   3 ☐   4 ☐   5 ☐

41. My home environment is full of clutter, and it's hard to find the things I need.

   1 ☐   2 ☐   3 ☐   4 ☐   5 ☐

42. I am a sensitive person, and I tend to take things personally, especially when it comes to my ex-spouse.

   1 ☐   2 ☐   3 ☐   4 ☐   5 ☐

43. I often think about what my ex is doing and who he/she is seeing, and I ask my children or common friends about him/her.

   1 ☐   2 ☐   3 ☐   4 ☐   5☐

44. On holidays, such as Christmas and New Year's, I feel somewhat down and lonely.

    1 □   2 □   3 □   4 □   5 □

45. I don't think that I'm responsible for my relationship breakup. It was all my ex's fault.

    1 □   2 □   3 □   4 □   5 □

Give yourself 1 point for each point you gave yourself. For example, if you ranked yourself as a 3 in one question, give yourself 3 points. Add up your total point score.

MY TOTAL SCORE: _____

Scoring Key

If you scored 90 points or less: Bravo! You have established a strong foundation as a single parent who will really support your children! You may fall into some of the pitfalls, but you don't stay in them long. Doing the exercises and action steps will help to solidify your skills and deepen your commitment to staying on the path that you're already on.

If you scored between 91–159 points: Good work! You are managing to avoid some of the single-parenting pitfalls and may be trapped in only a few of them. Those few pitfalls can be like quicksand, and it's important that you identify where you're feeling the most stuck and use the lessons and exercises in this book to climb out.

If you scored 160 points or more: Alert! Alert! You have fallen into a number of the single-parenting pitfalls! Give yourself an extra pat on the back for getting hold of this book, and it's time to get working! Your intentions may be good, but if you keep on this path, you are setting yourself and your children up for a rocky ride. You have some very black-and-white ideas about how things should go with your ex-spouse. You tend to take out your emotional issues on those around you. Playing the blame game may feel good in the short term, but in the long haul it leaves you feeling powerless and destined to be a victim of others.

✔ **Accountability Check**

☐   I will complete this exercise by: _____

☐   I completed this exercise on: _____

🎵 *Remember to Celebrate!* 🎵

Reminder

Come back after ninety days of working with the information in this book and retake your self-assessment quiz. See what's changed and celebrate your successes!

AFTER 90 DAYS, MY TOTAL SCORE IS: _____

✔ **Accountability Check**

☐   I will complete this exercise by: _____

☐   I completed this exercise on: _____

🎵 *Remember to Celebrate!* 🎵

Remember to record your actions in the "Take Action!" Tracker at the end of the book.

PART TWO

ESTABLISH A STRONG FOUNDATION

CHAPTER THREE

The THRIVE Principles™

"Smooth seas do not an experienced sailor make."

Anonymous

When you head out on a trip to a place you've never been before, do you take the time to get a map, some directions, or a compass to help you get there? Most people do. If you're traveling with children, you'll notice they always want to know "are we there yet?" or "how much longer?" Although your children won't ask these questions about the divorce process, they will experience the same sort of impatience for getting back into a routine or some semblance of "normalcy." Getting through the maze of divorce and learning to become a great single parent is going to be one of the most important journeys you can take in your life, so it's vital that you prepare properly.

I created my map the day I decided it wasn't good enough to simply "survive" or "get through" my divorce. For the sake of my children and myself, I chose to flourish and thrive instead. If life was going to hand me lemons, I was going to make some delicious lemonade!

I had a Masters degree in public policy from Harvard University and worked as a senior policy adviser and a fund-raising expert for many years. I was trained to give politicians, top-level bureaucrats, and administrators strategic advice, analysis, and policy recommendations. But when it came to steering my course through my divorce, I felt ill-prepared. My academic qualifications and professional experience didn't help me when it came to my own personal policy and direction. So I realized I needed to retrain myself. Equipped with the academic degrees to prove my intellectual ability, what I was lacking was training in emotional resiliency.

I started the process of reinventing and retraining myself, working with some of the best transformational and business trainers in the world. The drive to thrive propelled me through my healing and sparked the birth of my new company, Thrive After Divorce Inc. The company's mission is to empower people experiencing divorce to fearlessly create and express their highest potential. This chapter will give you the roadmap of the core principles you need to bring with you on your journey—the THRIVE Principles™.

The THRIVE Principles™

The THRIVE Principles™ have been fundamental to weathering any personal or professional storm I've encountered. The creation of the THRIVE Principles™ came to me during the course of writing this book. As I did my research, spoke to single parents, and reflected on my own experiences of divorce, I kept asking myself what was my motivating force that kept me going forward? What core values did I use as a compass to direct me on the road ahead? As I asked myself these questions, I kept hearing the word "thrive" and feeling the energy of that word resonate in my heart. The word itself conveys a sense of inspiration, hope and success. From this self-inquiry, I came to articulate what I call the THRIVE Principles™. As you'll see, each THRIVE Principle™ is a fundamental value or principle, configured together in an acronym that provides an easy frame of reference. These are not new principles. In fact, these universal principles and values have been taught by many great spiritual teachers and leaders over centuries of human existence. What is new, however, is the positioning of these core principles together.[10]

They are:

The THRIVE Principles™

Trust
Honesty
Responsibility
Integrity
Vision
Expression

T—Trust

The first principle is to TRUST. After divorce, your ability to trust others and yourself may be shattered. Divorce signifies the breakdown of trust in the partners at some level. For some, trust is broken in an obvious manner, such as infidelity or physical or emotional abuse. For others, trust is eroded more incrementally as partners grow apart and start taking each other for granted.

In order to trust others, we must first start with trusting ourselves. Author Stephen M. R. Covey argues that self-trust creates credibility and confidence. "Every time we make and keep a commitment to ourselves or set and achieve a meaningful goal, we become more credible," says Covey. "The more we do it, the more confidence we have that we can do it, that we will do it."[11]

Trust that you are made of the right stuff. Within yourself, you have every resource or skill you need to help you find your way through a problem. It's just a matter of learning how to access your own incredible talents.

Most importantly, we need to trust ourselves. You are the world's best expert on you, so please listen to yourself! Taking endless polls of other people's opinions only leads to analysis paralysis. Trust that you will make mistakes and that you can learn from them. When in doubt, simply take a deep breath, check in with your intuition, and trust where your heart wants to lead you.

You need to trust that your children will be healthy, happy, and capable of creating their own loving relationships. This may be hard, particularly at those moments when you see them unhappy, stressed, or confused. Trust that this relationship breakdown is part of a bigger picture that you cannot yet see.

Trust is a process of believing in yourself today, tomorrow, and the next day. It is a daily commitment you make to yourself. Trust that you can create healthy, intimate relationships in the future by choosing to learn from the mistakes of the past. Without trust in yourself, you are rudderless, and everything will feel difficult, confusing, or even scary. With trust, anything is possible.

H—Honesty

It's so important to learn to be HONEST with yourself and with others. Without honesty, there can be no authenticity. When you can be real with yourself and with others, they can be real with you. Clearly, a lack of honesty at some level plays a role in divorce.

This is an incredibly important lesson to teach our children. When we cover up our pain, our children sense that immediately. They then internalize the message, "I must learn to cover up my pain." Let's teach our children they don't have to be perfect little human beings. Let's teach them they are loved unconditionally for the human beings they are, complete with all their talents and flaws. We see their beauty and appreciate them for the treasures that they are in our lives.

To be honest and bare your heart to people leaves you vulnerable, which is why many people hedge their truth or hold back. Through our willingness and courage to be truly vulnerable, however, we can create relationships with greater intimacy and authentic connection.

In my own life, my connection with my children is far stronger than it was before my divorce and is a direct result, I believe, of my willingness to be honest and transparent with them. I express what's true for me, and they, in turn, feel safe and supported. They are willing to be honest with me and share what's true for them.

If you need help, be honest and ask for what you need. If you want to say no, be honest and decline. I'm always astonished how often people will say yes to a request just to be polite or "do the right thing" and then carry out the task with resentment and procrastination. Honesty is critical for business and personal partnerships of all kinds. Relationships built on honesty lead to more satisfaction and long-term success than those built on false pretenses.

R—Responsibility

The third principle is RESPONSIBILITY. As many great spiritual teachers tell us, we need to be 100 percent responsible for our current reality. We put ourselves in the driver's seat of our life only when we take 100 percent responsibility. Otherwise, we end up as the perpetual backseat driver—always knowing better after the fact.

When I first heard the concept of taking 100 percent responsibility at a personal-growth seminar I attended more than fifteen years ago, I was resistant and disbelieving. The seminar leader proposed that we are always 100 percent responsible for our reality, even in relationships. "I'm 100 percent responsible? That's not fair!" I groaned. I had thought that my ultimate goal in my relationship would be a fifty-fifty partnership, and therefore, I was only half responsible for the quality of my relationship.

As I struggled to try on this principle of 100 percent responsibility, I could see how much psychic energy I had spent evaluating that fifty-fifty equation on a regular basis. "Hey, today I put in about 75 percent, and you only put in 25 percent" would be the unconscious and unstated conclusion of how I would interact with my husband. Not being willing to take 100 percent responsibility left me blaming him and others. It left me feeling powerless because I let some portion of my happiness and well-being rest in the hands of other people, including my husband, to show up with their "50 percent" responsibility for the relationship. The truth of being 100 percent for myself and my happiness started to sink in.

Without responsibility, you are the powerless victim, spending your time and energy blaming others and making excuses for why you didn't get what you wanted in life. When you take responsibility, you are then able to make changes and take action to accomplish your goals. As I accepted that I was 100 percent responsible for the quality of my relationship, I began to feel a sense of relief and empowerment. I wasn't responsible for the actions or behaviors of others, but I was responsible for how I acted and behaved in response.

An often-overlooked component of responsibility is to distinguish the things you're responsible for from the things you are not responsible for. Women seem particularly skilled at taking responsibility for the emotional well-being and actions of others, while at the same time ignoring their responsibility to their own happiness and health. Before I truly understood and started living by this principle of responsibility, I had been a great believer in being compassionate with other people and caring for them. Unfortunately, I ignored my own needs to the point that I allowed myself to become a doormat in some of my important personal and business relationships. Using the principle of responsibility will help you to set clear and healthy boundaries in business and affairs of the heart.

It's never too early to introduce our children to the concept of responsibility. How many times has your child broken something or done something wrong, only to react with the stock "It's not my fault!" response? I know mine have. What I try to instill in my children is that it's important to be responsible for their own words and actions and that I expect them to be responsible for fixing their mistakes. Instead of crying over spilled milk, teach your children how to mop up the mess. This will take you out of the rescuer mode and support your children in becoming responsible and capable adults.

I—Integrity

One of the most fundamental principles is INTEGRITY. Your word is incredibly powerful and sets the universe in motion to align with your word. It's vital that you do what you say and say what you do. If you don't follow through on your word, whether it's your diet and exercise plan or making that call to your accountant, you are not honoring your word. Integrity has always been a fundamental value for me personally all my life, but my training as an integrative coach gave me a more complete appreciation for how powerful and fundamentally important this concept is.

Can you count on people who make promises to you and then don't follow through? Of course not! Yet that's the signal you give yourself every time you don't honor your own word: you can't count on you. You let yourself down. In fact, breaking promises to yourself is one way that you disrespect and devalue yourself. To thrive after divorce, you're going to need to count on you. Remember, actions speak louder than words.

When you're in integrity, you know it. A part of your vital life force gets snagged on whatever issue or relationship is out of integrity. Your mind engages in endless loops of inner dialogue that rationalize or justify why it's "okay" to not honor your word. It's like having a computer program running in the background, which slows your processing speed and sabotages your productivity. Being out of integrity chews up your psychic bandwidth.

If you don't honor your word, you must restore your integrity in order to get back into your flow. Fess up to yourself about the areas in your life in which you are not meeting your commitment. Either follow through or de-commit. As you extend your horizons, you have to keep raising the bar of your integrity.

Living in full integrity helps you to live "in the zone" where you'll find it effortless and magical to accomplish your goals.

In relationships, I've found integrity to be an invaluable yardstick in choosing my friends, clients, and business partners. Does someone call you when they say they will or follow through on their actions? If they don't, chances are that lack of integrity pervades their life more broadly. To thrive after divorce, you need a support system that is strong and unwavering. Dealing with people who are always out of integrity with you drains your precious energy. Use the integrity principle to create a safety net for yourself of people who have strong integrity as well.

V—Vision

Whether you're raising children, finding a relationship, building a trim body, or exploring a new hobby, you must take the time to create an inspiring VISION for yourself. This is particularly important for single parents who need to replace the old "happily ever after" vision with a new one that fits their current reality. It's an important principle, but it's also the first pitfall many single parents fall into.

Without a vision, we don't have the big picture. Multitasking, information overload, juggling overcrowded schedules, and high stress levels seem to characterize life in the twenty-first century. It's easy to get caught up in battling the daily brush fires, feeling like you can never get ahead. No wonder so many people feel like they're working harder than ever and can't enjoy the fruits of their labor.

Winston Churchill once said, "Never mistake the edge of your rut for the horizon." Articulating a vision defines your true horizon. Your vision should empower you and light you up from the inside. Holding a vision will pull you through the day-to-day challenges and keep you in action toward your goals. Being a great parent and creating a successful relationship with your ex-partner (if you so choose) will take every ounce of energy, creativity, and commitment that you have. That's why having a vision to fuel you and guide you is absolutely critical. We'll go into greater detail on the importance of vision and how you can create one in Chapter 4, "Pitfall #1: Not Having a Big Picture."

Articulating a new vision will also be a great support for your children. Most children do not fare well with uncertainties and unknowns. Letting them know you have a game plan will give them security and a sense of direction. You can even invite them to create it with you.

E—Expression

The final principle is EXPRESSION. Human beings have a huge range of emotional expression ranging from rage, sadness, and fear at one end of the spectrum to ecstasy and love at the other. Our *joie de vivre* comes when we can be our authentic selves and fully express ourselves. Young children can be our best teachers of this.

Divorce can cause you to clamp down on your self-expression. Sometimes people find themselves playing a role of "dutiful wife and mother" or "the guy who brings home the bacon." The ending of a marriage is an opportunity to break out of any old stereotypes and create a new expression of yourself.

You pay a price when you limit your emotional range. Growing up, I was very uncomfortable with anger, so I did everything I could to never feel that way. I would avoid conflict at all costs or try to please other people. But as I capped my risk of feeling those strong negative emotions, I also limited my ability to fully feel the joyous positive emotions that live at the other end of the spectrum.

As one of my teachers told me, emotion is simply energy in motion. Bottling up our emotions is like stuffing psychic sludge into your system. Eventually you either shut down, or you get backed up and explode. What I've learned is that expressing all of how I'm feeling is the best strategy I know for living fully and in the moment. You'll want to bring that energy and joy of life with you as you develop your life after divorce.

THRIVE Is a Mind-set

When you get divorced, imagining your life as a single parent can be daunting. Learning the ropes of being a successful single parent is like finding your way through a complex maze. Adopting the THRIVE Principles™ can help you find your way through the maze quickly, powerfully, and with ease.

The decision to simply "survive" or to "thrive" reflects the mind-set, attitudes, and beliefs you adopt. The ability for you and your children to flourish after divorce is something that starts from the inside and is then expressed outwardly. It starts in your attitude and in your heart first.

Now that we've clarified what each of the THRIVE Principles™ is, let's take a look at how they can make a difference in your mind-set. The table below illustrates how the THRIVE mind-set can take hold in your inner dialogue.

THRIVE Principles™	Choose to "Survive"	Choose to "Thrive"
TRUST	"I can't trust men/women anymore." "I'm so stupid—I can't trust myself." "I'll never, ever let myself be in this position again!" "I don't understand why these things happen to me."	"I trust I can handle anything." "I trust that everything happens for a reason." "I am open to learning from my past mistakes and trust I won't repeat them in the future." "I give myself the gift of self-trust."
HONESTY	"People won't like me or approve of me if I tell the truth." "It's not such a big deal—I'm over it already, honestly!" "A little white lie never hurt anyone." "Asking for help makes me feel weak and needy."	"It's OK to tell others that I'm scared or hurting." "I know that the truth sets me free." "I ask for help and support when I need it."
RESPONSIBILITY	"He/she did this to me." "It's not my fault my partner was a jerk." "My needs have to take a backseat to others, like my children, my family, and my friends." "I hate to be called selfish."	"I helped to create this situation." "I'm responsible for my own happiness." "My priority is to honor and love myself, first and foremost." "I honor the emotions and thoughts of others without the need to feel responsible for them or to try to fix them."
INTEGRITY	"I've got too much on my plate so it's OK that I don't follow through." "Everybody else seems to drop the ball on me and expects me to clean it up." "I try really hard to do what I say."	"I follow through on my commitments to others and to myself." "People can count on my word." "I am surrounded by people I can count on and trust." "Integrity is the compass I use in my life."

THRIVE Principles™	Choose to "Survive"	Choose to "Thrive"
VISION	"It seems like I go from one crisis to another." "I'm so busy, yet I never seem to get anywhere." "I don't feel like I make a difference." "I feel overwhelmed and scared when I think of my future."	"I feel fueled by a sense of purpose." "I believe each life event is preparation for my next step." "I like to step back and get the big picture." "I feel excited to create my future."
EXPRESSION	"I edit what I say before I speak." "I worry about what other people think of me." "I've got to keep myself together and be strong." "When I get into a funk, I don't know how to get out of it."	"I feel free to be me, even if I'm sad or angry." "I feel vibrant, alive, and happy with who I am." "Sometimes I feel like a kid at heart and act like one too!" "I'm comfortable expressing my emotions, and not only just the good ones."

You Deserve to Thrive

Each of us is here because we have a unique talent or gift we bring to the world. You are blessed with your children. Use the THRIVE Principles™ as the foundation for living your life and delivering what you have to offer to your children and the world with passion, joy, and ease!

You can easily teach and model each of the principles to your children. Review the THRIVE Principles™ again, this time considering whether you feel these principles are important for your children to learn. I think you'll agree with me that the THRIVE Principles™ represent a great cornerstone for creating a happy and inspired future.

Take Action!

1. Write the THRIVE Principles™ out on a separate piece of paper or index card so you can post them where you'll see them often.

✔ # Accountability Check

☐   I will complete this exercise by: _____

☐   I completed this exercise on: _____

♫ *Remember to Celebrate!* ♪

2. For each principle, create a personal affirmation to reinforce the THRIVE Principles™. Be sure you state the affirmation in the present tense, as if it is already happening.

Examples:

Trust	I trust I can handle any situation with ease and grace.
Honesty	I am honest with myself and others.
Responsibility	I am responsible for my own happiness.
Integrity	I have integrity, and people know they can count on me to do what I say.
Vision	I have a vision of my children and me having a loving, connected relationship.
Expression	I express myself fully each day.

Visit www.7pitfalls.com to download a free copy of affirmations based on the THRIVE Principles™. You can also download a blank affirmation template to fill with your own affirmations and post as a reminder.

Take Action!

MY PERSONAL THRIVE AFFIRMATIONS

TRUST _____

_____

_____

HONESTY _____

_____

_____

RESPONSIBILITY _____

_____

_____

INTEGRITY _____

_____

_____

VISION _____

_____

_____

EXPRESSION _____

_____

_____

Take Action!

 Accountability Check

☐   I will complete this exercise by: _____

☐   I completed this exercise on: _____

♪ *Remember to Celebrate!* 🎤

Remember to record your actions in the "Take Action!" Tracker at the end of the book.

PART THREE

THE 7 PITFALLS

CHAPTER FOUR

Pitfall #1: Not Having a Big Picture

"Destiny grants us our wishes, but in its own way, in order to give us something beyond our wishes."

Johann Wolfgang von Goethe

Have you heard the expression, "It's easy to lose sight of the forest for the trees"? Without creating a big picture for our lives (the forest), it's easy to get stuck in the daily issues of being a single parent (the trees). All parents have a lot on their plates, but single parents have additional responsibilities. For you, life can be a blur of managing your children, rebuilding your life, dealing with your ex, and coping with your career. It's easy to become overwhelmed and lose your bearings.

At the beginning of life as a single parent, the big picture might just be getting through the day. Your vision, your next step might be to get through the holiday season without major emotional upset. One pitfall many single parents make is failing to establish what they'd like their new life to look and feel like. It's critical to stop and create a new vision for yourself.

Signs That You're Stuck

- **You feel like you're always reacting and putting out fires.** You feel overwhelmed and find yourself reacting defensively to situations, even if they are situations you've faced before. You are impatient and frustrated. You feel little sense of progress in how you and your children are coping with the divorce.
- **Your game plan is survival.** Your biggest ambition is to simply survive the day. The idea of thriving after your divorce seems like a pie-in-the-sky idea. You feel powerless and thoughts of "why is this happening to me?" are common. Your plan is to simply put one foot in front of the other and hope that you don't get knocked off your feet along the way.
- **You feel like you've lost your bearings.** You feel awash in a totally new situation with your divorce, and it's hard to know where you're headed. You feel ill-suited to helping your children navigate this new territory because you really don't know where you're headed. You are confused, and there is no consistent context for the decisions you make. The future looks unclear and uncertain to you.
- **Your mood and energy level is low.** You often wake up in the morning feeling tired or listless. You may wake up in the night with lots of thoughts or worries and find it difficult to get back to sleep. You feel like your inner reserves of energy, strength, and resiliency are low.

Without having the big picture in mind, it's easy to get bogged down in the challenges that life will throw your way every day. Without a vision, the first hurdle you encounter—whether it's a late child-support payment, a school concert which you and your ex both attend, or another meeting with the lawyers—will feel insurmountable unless you know where you want to go.

A Personal Perspective

One afternoon, in the midst of my separation, I had sunk to a deep level of despair. My stomach was in knots, and my mind was racing with worries and fears. "Oh my God, what is my life going to be like when I'm divorced?" I wondered. It was very clear to me that I was heading into the deep, dark, unknown waters of divorce. I questioned how I would survive. I was consumed with anxiety about my children's fate. Each negative thought seemed to whip up another level of overwhelm, guilt, and shame. It seemed for the first time in my life that I was confronted with a challenge that I simply couldn't "figure out," Harvard graduate degree notwithstanding. The vision of a long and happy marriage that I'd held for twenty years was clearly over, and I had no clue what was next for me.

Then a thought came into my head. "Well, it seems I'm going down a road I never expected, and I don't know what's ahead," I told myself. "But I give up. I don't know where I'm going, but I'm willing to see where this path takes me." As soon as I articulated those thoughts, an incredible shift took place within me. Suddenly I felt all of the anxious knots and tightness drain from my body. I was filled with a sense of calm, peace, and spaciousness. I felt lighter, hopeful, and even curious about the adventure that lay ahead of me. I have to say that since that day years ago, I have carried that sense of inner peace with me.

After my moment of surrender, I started to ask myself questions and could hear the answers of my small, wise voice start to answer me. What could my life look like? What kind of relationship do I want to have with my children? How do I want to feel about myself? What kind of partner would I like to have for a future relationship?

By surrendering and asking myself questions, a new vision has come forth. My initial vision was of being the best mom I could be. I saw myself becoming a woman free to express herself and play full out in her life. I saw myself as an inspiration to my children and as an example to others of how to love themselves. My vision has blossomed into being of service to thousands of other single parents by sharing my own experience and knowledge. It is from my vision this book was born.

The Impact on Your Children

When you're feeling reactive, low in energy, and uncertain about what your future looks like, your children will pick up on that and likely magnify it. Your children look to you for guidance and reassurance that they will always be loved and safe. Children will follow the example that you set. So if you feel like life is unfair because it's always giving you the short straw, your children will model that behavior. One way to create a vision for your life is to do so with your children.

Putting the Pieces of Your Life's Jigsaw Puzzle Back Together

Have you ever tried to put together a jigsaw puzzle without having the lid that shows you the whole picture? It's frustrating and unsatisfying. As you look at all those individual pieces, you know they could make a nice picture if you could just put them together the right way. Without a picture guiding you, you feel overwhelmed and incompetent. If you happen to put part of the puzzle together, it's really through chance, not through choice.

Creating a vision for your family after divorce is like finding the lid to the puzzle box that shows you how the picture can look for you. When you were married, you had already put together a lot of the pieces in your life's puzzle. But now, the part of the picture showing you being happily married to your spouse has changed. Having your children thrive after divorce requires you to create and claim a new vision and take the steps to put a new puzzle together.

Let's take this analogy of putting together the pieces of a puzzle a little bit further. If you were handed the pieces of a jigsaw puzzle but not given the lid, what would you do? Would you sit down and tell yourself, "I guess I'm just not meant to complete jigsaw puzzles" or "There must be something wrong with me if I can't put this puzzle together"? Or how about, "This stupid company. It's their fault I don't have the lid, and they probably did that on purpose!" Of course not! Most people would look at the pieces and say, "Gee, it would be a lot easier to put this together if I could find that lid!" and start searching for it. Or they would put the puzzle aside and work on one that had a picture they liked.

But that's not what many of us do when we separate. We beat ourselves up for the failed relationship in some way, whether we initiated the divorce or not. We feel victimized by it or vindicated that here, finally, is the proof that all of our worst fears about ourselves are true: "There is something wrong with me, I don't deserve love, and I don't know how to get what I most want." Creating a vision will pull you forward with clarity and inspiration on how to put the puzzle pieces of your life back together in the way you want.

Creating a Vision

Start first with creating a new vision for yourself. You had the vision of you as a couple, married happily ever after. When you become a single parent, it's important to create a new vision and replace it with a new picture for yourself.

Otherwise, you'll unconsciously keep judging and comparing your current reality against that old vision of "happily ever after." You'll end up feeling disappointed and dissatisfied. It's best to start first with a vision for yourself, both as an individual and as a parent. After you've got that in place, you can create a family vision with your children.

You and your ex will be coparents for as long as you have children. This is all the more reason to take some time to brainstorm and create a vision for your life. Start off by thinking about what you'd like your relationship between yourself and your ex-spouse to look like in five, ten, or twenty years. Don't let yourself be constrained by the current state of your relationship. You also don't need to limit your brainstorming process by wondering how exactly you'll get there. Take a moment to clear your mind, take a deep breath, and start with a blank slate. Then ask yourself, "What is my vision for my life—with my children and with my ex-spouse?"

To assist you, imagine that it is several years down the road and your first child is about to graduate from high school or get married, or your first grandchild has been born. What do you want that day to look and feel like? Do you want to be able to enjoy that important milestone with a sense of pride, accomplishment, and celebration? Do you want your child to feel a sense of ease with having both birth parents participate in this special day? Or do you want to protect yourself from having anything to do with your ex-spouse and just hope you can grit your teeth and get through the experience so you won't disappoint your child?

Clearly these two visions have been set out at different ends of the spectrum to illustrate a point. Your vision may be somewhere in between. Your vision may not necessarily be that you and your ex hoist a glass together to celebrate that first grandchild. Perhaps your vision is that you can be in the same room and be respectful and not resentful of him/her. Write down in as much detail as you can the vision you start to create for yourself.

Five Components of a Vision

Vision is a powerful tool for everyone, from single parents to CEOs and everyone in between. Businesses, governments, and other large institutions spend millions of dollars creating their vision and then articulating it to their stakeholders: employees, shareholders, clients, and voters. A vision ensures that all team members are on the same page and work toward that big picture. Yet how much time do we as individuals, or as families, spend creating a vision of how we want to live? Isn't your life worth spending some time and energy on to reflect and create your own vision?

A vision is the end picture you are working toward for yourself and your children. It is a possible future for your family. Your vision is an expression of the intention you set for how you will create your life as a single parent. There are five key components to a powerful vision:

1. **It defines what is truly important to you.** Your vision is an expression of your core values. Your values determine your priorities and guide your actions, thoughts, and goals. You express your values in how you live your life every day. Your values might include honesty, integrity, love, open-mindedness, and creativity.

2. **Your vision creates a destination.** Leadership and organizational expert Stephen Covey advises that we "start with the end in mind." A vision articulates where you want to end up. This is critical because without a clear destination in mind, the chances of you ever getting there are between slim and none. Think about planning a trip without a destination. How do you plan your route, what to pack, and what currency you'll need to bring if you have no idea whether you're going to Paris, the Antarctic, or the Midwest?

3. **You can feel it.** A powerful vision has an emotional element to it. You can imagine clearly how that vision looks and feels. You can see the faces of the people surrounding you as you live your vision. Our brain thinks in images, not words, so your vision can be drawn out of your imagination, and you'll feel a rush of energy in your body as your vision lights you up. Thoughts, beliefs, and interpretations are a natural byproduct of getting connected to your vision. A human being always acts and feels and performs according to what he *imagines* to be *true* about himself and his environment. This is why hypnotized people can develop blisters when they're told they've been burned.

4. **Your vision acts like a magnet.** When you are connected to your vision and feel lit up by it, you will be able to feel that vision pulling you forward, like a magnet. Day-to-day issues will always be there, but the vision is so compelling that you'll do whatever is necessary to move through the daily grind to keep on the path toward that vision. Your vision adds a new and broader perspective and context to your life.

5. **Visions are the bird's eye view.** Visions are broad and open ended. Your vision gives you a picture of the forest, giving you a broader perspective than just the individual trees in the forest. The emotional experience of living your vision is what's important. The specifics of exactly how

you'll get there are part of your goal-setting process to move toward the vision. Visions can also be changed or revised as you move toward them.

The Benefits of Vision

There are numerous benefits to having a vision for yourself:

1. **You create instead of react.** Rather than reacting, a vision allows you to create your life in a much more conscious way. Instead of operating on autopilot and default mode, you make conscious and deliberate decisions and choices.[12] Every day you make thousands of choices that, over time, will determine the future you experience. By asking yourself "Does this choice take me in the direction of my vision or away from it?" you take charge of your life.
2. **Your vision is your compass.** Anyone who has hiked in the wilderness knows how valuable and lifesaving a compass is. No matter how disoriented or lost you may become, your compass unfailingly tells you where north is. Your vision acts like a compass guiding you forward in the face of competing priorities and rocky relationships. If you "start with the end in mind," you will clearly see what battles you'll want to fight and which ones you should concede. Your priorities are aligned with your vision. You focus your time and energy on the issues that move you toward your vision.
3. **Visions are tools to build agreement.** Articulating a vision to yourself is powerful. Sharing it with your children or with others in your family gives it even more potency. The process of creating a vision is a great way to build agreement with your children. They will also gain a sense of ownership, responsibility, and power as they participate in creating a family vision. Your vision is also a declaration to the world of what you see for yourself. It's like creating your personal billboard advertisement to the universe of what you're willing to receive.
4. **A vision improves communication and establishes a sense of teamwork.** Creating a vision is a wonderful way to build a strong team spirit in your family. Remember the jigsaw puzzle and all the different pieces? Everyone has a unique piece of the puzzle to bring. When you put them all together, you can see the whole picture. Everyone in the family will have a better understanding of how their role impacts the overall vision.

Harness the Law of Attraction

There are many examples of individuals who held a vision and didn't let challenges along the way stop them. Think of Martin Luther King Jr. or Mahatma Gandhi, to name but two. In fact, their visions inspired others to join them in making their dreams a reality. In the words of Johann Wolfgang von Goethe, "Whatever you can do, or dream you can, begin it. Boldness has genius, power, and magic in it."

Brain science supports why visualization is so important. We are exposed to millions and millions of bits of information each day, and part of our brain sorts out what parts are important to us and what are not. We become conscious and aware of the important pieces of information, such as the empty fuel gauge warning in our car or our child's scream of pain. We are not aware of the color of our neighbor's cat or the turnoff to a town we aren't planning to visit. When we connect to our vision, we start to tune that same part of our brain into the reality we want to create. It's like tuning a radio into a particular frequency in order to best hear the music you like. Our brain will comply by searching for reality that matches the image we're holding. It starts to filter and notice those bits of information that will help us create our vision.

This is the Law of Attraction: we attract into our lives whatever we focus on. What you focus on and put out there is exactly what you'll get. Imagine that the universe is like a big short-order diner. You've got God, spirit, your higher self, or whatever you want to call it in the back as the short-order cook. "Yup, Dolores is sure her ex-husband will try to stiff her on child support again this month. Coming right up!" So Dolores, did you want a side order of fries with that too? Or the man who worries that he'll never be able to trust women again. The universal short-order cook fires up the grill with, "Hey, let's send this guy a new girlfriend to break his heart so he can be right about that!"

The Law of Attraction is not a recent New Age concept, but is derived from the physical laws of science and has been documented and written about throughout the twentieth century. Electrons orbit the nucleus of an atom in prescribed orbits that vary depending on the energy. When electrons receive energy, they shift to a higher orbit. When energy is taken away, the electrons shift to a lower orbit. If atoms are at a similar vibrational level, "they create a motive force, all pulling together in the same direction in much the same way as metals can be magnetized by aligning their molecules in the same direction," explains Law of Attraction expert and author, Michael Losier.[13]

When you feel yourself fuelled by your vision, you alter your vibrational state and will start to attract things that are a match for your vibrational state. As Losier says, the Law of Attraction "is a law of nature that every atom of your being is in constant response to, whether you know it or not." The Law of Attraction is wonderfully illustrated and explained in the movie, *The Secret*, which I highly recommend. Visit www.thesecret.tv to learn more. For more on the Law of Attraction, please see the Recommended Resources section of this book.

Take Action!

1. To create a powerful vision, the most important place to start is in your relationship with yourself. Imagine your first child is getting married or graduating from school. It's a big family celebration for your child. To get yourself started with your new vision, consider the following questions:
    - How do you want to feel?

    _____

    _____

    _____

    _____

    _____

    _____

Take Action!

- How will you treat yourself?

  _____

  _____

  _____

  _____

  _____

- How are your children feeling?

  _____

  _____

  _____

  _____

  _____

- What kind of relationship do you have with your children? With your ex-spouse?

  _____

  _____

  _____

  _____

  _____

Take Action!

- What kind of friends and relationships will you have?

_____

_____

_____

_____

_____

_____

- How will you support yourself physically? emotionally? spiritually?

_____

_____

_____

_____

_____

_____

Take Action!

- What new beliefs and behaviors do you have that allow you to live in that vision?

_____

_____

_____

_____

_____

_____

_____

Spend thirty minutes reflecting on these questions, and jot down your insights.

✔ Accountability Check

☐   I will complete this exercise by: _____

☐   I completed this exercise on: _____

♪ *Remember to Celebrate!* ♪

---

2.   Write at least one page on your new vision. Just let it flow initially and feel free to use exciting and inspiring adjectives. You can edit it after you've got your first draft done. Reading your vision should inspire and motivate you.

Take Action!

MY INSPIRING NEW VISION

Take Action!

 Accountability Check

☐   I will complete this exercise by: _____

☐   I completed this exercise on: _____

♫ *Remember to Celebrate!* 🎤

Remember to record your actions in the "Take Action!" Tracker at the end of the book.

CHAPTER FIVE

Pitfall #2: Getting Hooked by Your Ex-spouse

"Always forgive your enemies; nothing annoys them so much."

Oscar Wilde

Have you ever been totally triggered and emotionally hijacked by something your ex said or did? Have you ever been totally triggered and hijacked by something your ex didn't say or do? I'm hoping you just answered yes to those questions, so I'm not the only divorced parent out there who has felt that way!

To make sure we're on the same page, let's define what I mean by being "hooked by" or "plugged in" to your ex-spouse. When you're plugged in to the actions of someone else, you typically have a strong emotional reaction and a very strong opinion that you are *right* and the other person is absolutely *wrong*. It's interesting that the phrase is "plugged in," because that it what it feels like. It's as if you have some kind of outlet or opening that allows the other to come right in, like plugging a wire into an electrical socket, and *zap*—you're gone.

You are wired up to that person, who hijacks your emotions and drains a lot of your time and energy.

Do you find it hard to be the kind of parent you want to be when you're feeling like that? I know I do. Wouldn't it be wonderful if you could consistently parent your children from a connected and loving place? If you want to learn how to defuse some of those volatile emotions so you can stop taking out the frustrations you have with your ex-partner on your children, this chapter is for you.

Signs That You're Stuck

- **Your emotions run high.** You feel strong emotions, such as anger, resentment, blame, or fear. These emotions feel "hot" to handle, which is exactly where common phrases like "in the heat of the moment" and "in the heat of battle" come from. As emotions run high, the ability to think rationally runs low. Some people feel like they've been hijacked by their emotions, leaving them wondering, "Did I really say that?" or "I can't believe I actually did that!"

- **You are reactive.** When you're hooked, you react out of instinct. Instead of getting creative and trying to solve the problem, your old reptilian brain usually fires up some of the fight-or-flight neurons in your system. With all of those neurological defense systems activated, the ability to calmly reflect and consider alternative courses of actions takes a nosedive. Everything is black or white, right or wrong, and you are not willing to tolerate dissenting views.

- **Let the blame game begin.** You start to blame your ex-spouse. The laundry list of current and past grievances starts pouring out of your mind or your mouth as you create a bulletproof case of how your ex-spouse is absolutely *wrong* and you are absolutely *right*.

- **You climb up on the soap box.** With your prepared case of how you are victimized by your ex-spouse, you argue your case to whomever you can. This is commonly known as gossip. You plead your case with righteous conviction, and you are unwilling to hear alternative views.

- **You have negative, repetitive thoughts.** You experience a repeating pattern of internal dialogue. "Man, when she said this, I should have done that. And then she would have never tried what she tried." It's like having the record needle stuck in a scratch on your record. (For those of you who never had the joy of experiencing vinyl record albums firsthand, trust me on this one—it's tedious and annoying.)

- **You waste time and energy.** When that initial surge of adrenaline hits the bloodstream, being hooked can seem energizing. But in reality, it's an energy drain. When you're hooked into another person, a huge amount of time and emotional energy is wrapped up in that drama. The other person doesn't even have to be in the room—or in the country, for that matter—but when you get hooked, they can suck your life force. Ironically, the person you publicly proclaim you're "over with" ends up consuming your thoughts, time, energy, and peace of mind.

Your Ex Knows How to Push Your Buttons

In the breakup of an intimate relationship, you move through many layers of "detangling." Over the years of your relationship, you likely developed emotional closeness and compassion, caring deeply about the happiness and well-being of your partner. In fact, you cared so much about each other that you chose to have children together.

As that relationship breaks up, it takes a while for you to unhook yourself from the emotional connection that characterized your partnership. Have you noticed your former partner seems to know exactly what buttons to push to drive you absolutely around the bend? How does he or she know the exact thing to say or do, or the exact thing to not say or not do, that will knock you off balance and send you into a foul mood? Is it just because your ex is being vindictive, or is it because you have remained emotionally hooked into your ex-spouse?

It is highly likely that when you were married or living together, your partner would find ways to "push your buttons" and vice versa. Within the context of being in a committed relationship, there is a willingness to work through these emotional issues together. Within the context of divorce, there typically isn't the desire or the structure to work through these issues together, so the responsibility to sort out your emotional flashpoints with your ex-spouse lies with you.

If the relationship with your ex-spouse feels difficult, it indicates that there's still work to do and issues to be healed, says author Debbie Ford. "We must heal our inner wounds. If we don't do it, we keep fueling the conflict and the hurt."[14]

To move forward and create new loving relationships in the future, it's important to get to a sense of completion with your former partner. The breakdown of the relationship, whether you initiated it or not, creates a shock to your system. "It's important to emotionally release the pain and anger," advises intimacy expert Vered Neta.[15] The form of emotional release will depend on the individual. "Without completion, you'll start new relationships while still carrying a remnant of your old relationship." To release those energetic remnants, Neta recommends finding a strategy that works for the kind of person you are. "Some people are more physical, so running like hell on a beach and screaming is a great way to release negative and painful emotions," she says. "Others may be more suited to journaling about their feelings and thoughts quietly. It's important that you allow yourself to cry and grieve the loss of the relationship." According to Neta, completion has more to do with yourself, not your former partner. "Ask yourself, where did I grow? What did my partner contribute to me? Most importantly," she urges, "take the time to acknowledge yourself."

Right now, take a moment to evaluate, on a scale of 1–10, how plugged in you typically are to your ex. If you're never plugged into your ex, give yourself a 1. If you feel extremely agitated and plugged into your ex on a daily basis, give yourself a 10. When you first separate, you'll likely find yourself in the 7–10 range. I recommend using this simple technique to take a reading on your emotional state. Over time, and with greater life experience, you will see that number drop, and one day, you'll even be able to consciously shift it.

The Cost to Your Children

Very often, particularly in the early stages of separation and divorce, it's very easy to simply react to your former partner—the things your ex does (or doesn't do), how he or she says things, or his or her personal habits. You get upset when agreements are broken, or you get angry when your former partner brings a new love interest home to meet your children. "He is just so self-centered," Amanda fumed about her former husband. "Of course, he was an hour late picking up the kids, just like he always was, and I'm left answering their questions as to why Daddy was late!" When you parent from a reactive state, you risk spilling some of your toxic emotions of frustration and anger at your ex-spouse onto your children.

Here's an analogy that I find useful to remember when I think about how being hooked into my ex-husband affects my parenting. Do you remember the "olden days" when you used to have to turn the radio dial to go from one station to the next? Imagine that your children are on a frequency that is the next radio station. As a parent, you want to tune into that station so you get a clear, strong signal and can hear the music of your children. When you are plugged in to strong emotions or unresolved issues related to your ex-spouse, you encounter static in your tuner. All of a sudden, it's hard to tune into your kids because of all of the interference. Listening to static gets irritating pretty quickly!

What happens when your unresolved issues, energy, and emotions regarding your ex enter into the parenting arena? It creates static in your relationship with your child. It shows up in how you parent your children in the following ways:

- **You're not present.** Your body may be there in front of your child, but *you* are not there. Your mind and heart are off somewhere else, hashing it out with your ex-partner.
- **You're not available for your child.** How do you feel when you try to speak with or connect to someone when they are distracted by someone or something else? Do you feel like you're not being heard? Do you feel like you're not important enough to warrant their attention? That's exactly what happens to your child when you're hooked.
- **The connection between you and your child is broken.** You'll have static in your communication channels with your child. Children are like intuitive sponges, and they pick up everything, even if it's not verbal. They pick up on your tone, your energy, and your mood. They can feel the disconnect between themselves and you.
- **Children feel powerless and confused.** When your parenting becomes inconsistent and unpredictable because you're hooked by your ex-spouse, your children feel like they're walking on eggshells. They pick up on the tension you feel, which leaves them feeling unsettled and frightened.

The bottom line is that your children need to make sense of your behavior, and they will make it mean something about them. If they see you distracted or upset, they may conclude they've done something wrong or your emotional state is somehow their fault.

Your children also may start to model your behavior. Children will do what you do, not what you say. So if they see you with a short temper that flares up unpredictably, or watch you roll your eyes and sigh at the mention of your ex-spouse, chances are high they'll follow your lead.

Strategies to Get Unhooked

It is important to parent from a neutral place. You need to be able to speak to your children from a clear, connected place without the static of your judgments of their other parent in the way. The impact of being hooked by your ex-spouse affects your tone, your body language, your listening, your attitude, and your energy level. You need to adopt five key strategies to stop getting hooked by your ex-partner:

1.   Realize that what your ex thinks of you is none of your business.
2.   Take responsibility for your reality, and focus on what's under your control.
3.   Reframe your relationship with your ex-spouse and adopt a business partnership model.
4.   Create a supportive environment.
5.   Don't rely solely on a legal solution.

1.   What Your Ex Thinks of You Is NONE of Your Business

As you shift from a romantic/intimate relationship with your ex-spouse into a more business-like partnership that focuses on raising your children together successfully, you must start to pull out the emotional hooks that you have embedded in your psyche. The most important mantra you can use is: "**What my ex thinks of me is none of my business.**" Yes, that's right—to have emotional freedom and to take full responsibility for your life, the most important shift in awareness that you can make is to realize that what your former spouse thinks of you is absolutely none of your business.

You must choose to not take the actions of your ex-spouse personally. Don Miguel Ruiz, author of *The Four Agreements*, says that "not taking anything personally does not mean that you will not have a reaction or you will not take action. But when you take action, you have clarity, you know exactly what you want. When you take things personally, you do things you don't want to do and say things you don't want to say, because emotions are controlling you."[16]

Notice how you feel about this idea right now. Do you feel yourself resisting it? "But I want him to understand what I'm doing so he doesn't sabotage me!" "She's going to bad-mouth me all over town, so I have to manage my risk!" If you're hearing a lot of inner dialog welling up in opposition, that means right now you're actually pretty committed to spending a lot of your emotional and psychic energy in an area you have absolutely no control over. Does this sound like a good strategic choice to you?

Let's face it—most of us were raised to believe that to be a "good girl" or a "good boy" we needed to care about other people's feelings. Yes, it is important to have respect for their feelings and not to be callous and deliberately vindictive with others. However, many of us have gone too far in taking responsibility for other people's feelings and emotional well-being. This seemingly "kind" act actually has a number of potentially destructive outcomes.

When you make what other people think or feel about you more important than what you think or feel about yourself, you feel dissatisfied and ultimately resentful. You withhold communicating something important to you because you worry they might "take it the wrong way" or become upset. Instead, you erect a barrier that prevents you from being truly authentic and available to this person. Is this the kind of connection you want to create with people you say you care about?

Needing to please others, to have them approve of you or "like" you, victimizes you. You set yourself up for feeling powerless in your own life. In a way, you also victimize the person you're trying to please. They don't get to relate to the real you, and they build their connection to you on a false premise.

Now take a look at how this plays out specifically with your former spouse. Ask yourself why you wouldn't want to make the fact that what your ex thinks of you is none of your business as your personal motto. Do you want your ex to like you? To agree with you? To understand you perhaps? People spend a lot of time and energy looking at their ex-spouses. "How could she treat me like this?" "What is going on that he could say something like that in front of the children?" We spend a lot of time and energy getting other people to see it our way as well. After all, we'd rather be right than happy.

Be honest with yourself—did your ex like, respect, or agree with you when you were married? Chances are, not enough, otherwise you might not be divorced now. If your ex-partner didn't "get" you or respect you when you were married, how is that suddenly going to turn around now that you're divorced?

Worrying and getting upset about what your ex-spouse will think or feel or say about you is simply a habitual distraction that you use to avoid looking at how *you* feel about your situation and seeing what *you* need to do. Will your former partner ever think a negative thought about you, get upset about something you've done, or bad-mouth you to other people? Absolutely. You're divorced, and most likely not happy with each other all the time, right? Is there anything you can do to prevent that? Who knows? If you try to go on the offensive and start retaliating in some way, you're just engaging in a power struggle that will take you nowhere fast and leave you feeling bitter and exhausted. The likely victims from that power struggle will be your children.

The only thing you do have control over is you—the thoughts you think, the actions you take, the things you say, and the feelings you have. Your ex-spouse can worry about how he or she feels about you. Your ex-spouse is a grown-up and can take care of him- or herself. Law of Attraction expert Michael Losier offers a useful update to the adage of "mind your own business." He defines the Law of Attraction as: "I attract to my life whatever I give my attention, energy and focus to, whether positive or negative."[17] He teaches his students to "mind your own vibration" because otherwise you'll start attracting more of the dynamics you don't want in your life.

After you start focusing on what you feel about yourself and what you need to do, you can reclaim some of the energy you've been frittering away worrying about things you have no control over. That's when things have the possibility of turning around. You gain so much freedom in letting go of the fantasy that your ex should behave, act, or think in a certain way. Suffering comes when your fantasy is different from the reality you're living. The ironic thing is that after you let your fantasy go and start taking responsibility for what you do have control over, that's probably when your ex will start to behave differently.

2.   Take Responsibility for Your Reality

Remember the THRIVE Principles™ that we started with? The R is for responsibility. The bottom line is that is you are only responsible for your own feelings, emotions, behaviors, actions, and thoughts. Ultimately, those are the only pieces of your life over which you have any iota of control.

You are not responsible for other people's feelings, emotions, behaviors, actions, and thoughts. You are not responsible for their emotional experiences or judgments. When you play the game of being responsible for things that are beyond your control, you'll lose every time and become miserable in the process.

In the midst of my separation process, I was talking to a wise friend of mine and complaining about how unreasonable my former husband had apparently become now that we were talking about nuts and bolts issues, like asset division and money. She said, "If he didn't get you or appreciate you when you were married, why are you expecting him to do that when you are divorcing?" Wham! New perspective!

If you're feeling stuck in old patterns with your ex, ask yourself the following question: How will I live a great life even if my ex never supports, agrees with, or acknowledges me? Don't let your happiness and self-esteem hinge on something your ex may never be willing or able to give you. Choose to thrive after divorce and do your best for yourself, with or without the support of your former partner.

Ask yourself what you need, and then give it to yourself. Name it—if your ex isn't being respectful, is there some place in your life where you need to give yourself greater respect? When your ex doesn't follow through as promised, is there some issue where you are not following through as promised? Our relationships with our former partners often offer the biggest clues to us as to how we can move forward and take responsibility for creating our results.

3.   Reframe Your Relationship with Your Ex

Becoming a single parent requires you to redesign the relationship you have with the mother or father of your children. At one point in your lives, you were in love with each other, excited to create a family together, and engaged in living your version of "happily ever after." Although the marriage has ended, the job of being a parent has not. So it's critical that you take a step back and decide what you'd like that parenting partnership to look like. Out of the ashes of a failed marriage arises the opportunity to create a new relationship with your former spouse.

Your relationship with your ex will need to change from an emotional and romantic relationship to more of a business partnership. Imagine you are both cofounders and CEOs of the business of raising healthy and emotionally well-adjusted children. As in any business partnership, your mission, expectations, agreements, job descriptions, and boundaries need to be explicit and negotiated. Your communications will need to be structured. Meetings will be much smoother if you work from an agenda, rather than view each interaction as an opportunity to reopen old wounds.

It's not always easy to be great coparents, and yet that is a gift well worth giving to your children.

4.   Create a Supportive Environment

Thomas Leonard, the founding father of the personal coaching profession, wrote about the importance of your environment. Your environment includes physical and social structures. When you choose to thrive after divorce, ensure that your external environment can support and enhance that choice.

Is there a feeding frenzy with friends or family, wanting to engage in gossip or ex bashing with you? Initially, this may feel good to you and satisfy any feelings of revenge that you may have. In the long run, it will do you and your children no good. You don't move forward when you blame or make others wrong. You actually perpetuate and strengthen your relationship with your ex-spouse, but in a very detrimental way that makes you a victim.

It's important that you create a supportive environment for yourself, knowing that divorce propels you through a major life transition. Like a snake needs to shed a layer of skin, you may need to shed some old friends or habits that don't support your growth and healing. "Sometimes your friends aren't the best people for support," advises best-selling author Debbie Ford. "We train our friends how to be with us. They all have agendas, righteous positions, and opinions. At a time of pain, they might just give back the reflection of our old selves. What's wanting to be birthed is a new creation of ourselves. It's imperative that we surround ourselves with people willing to have and see and allow a new version to be birthed, rather than people who will support us in our old story." [18]

You may need to retrain your support people. Surround yourself with people who understand your desire to change the old dynamics of your relationship with your ex. Let your supporters know you are making a few changes, such as:

- **The pity party is over.** Tell your social circle you've decided to stop wallowing in the past and are ready to move forward. Tell them you've chosen to thrive after divorce, and coos of sympathy and expressions of "poor you" don't work for you anymore.
- **Implement a "no gossip" policy.** Tell your supporters that you've decided to take responsibility for your thoughts, words, and actions. You've decided that from now on you plan to speak to the person who can take action on your issues. Let them know you'll no longer talk behind other people's backs to third parties. Advise them that you won't participate in gossip fests with them about other people either.
- **Appreciate their support.** When you decide to unplug from your ex, you might find that some of your supporters will feel like they no longer know how to support you. To continue to feel connected to you, they may want you to plug in again so they feel they have a purpose and relationship with you. A great remedy is to appreciate them wholeheartedly for their past sympathy and support. Let them know you plan to divert the energy you might have spent gossiping toward more positive endeavors and creating your future.
- **Alter your environment.** You may find that some people in your environment continue to drain your energy like vampires, even if you've

laid out your ground rules. You will have to let go of some people to move on. Make yourself less available to your "energy vampires" and find other positive influences for yourself.

5.   Don't Rely Solely on a Legal Solution

You are ultimately responsible for your relationship with your ex-spouse. Some single parents make the mistake of relying on the court system and lawyers to hammer out a working relationship between the two parties. In cases of physical threat or abuse, the courts, child welfare agencies, or the police need to be called in to intervene. However, it can be a costly mistake to assume that the family law courts will positively impact your coparenting relationship with your ex-spouse.

When I got separated, I assumed that after I hired a lawyer everything would get sorted out. My lawyer would figure out the best custody arrangements, the best financial settlement, and the best way to handle any future disputes.

While most lawyers are highly trained, ethical people, they get paid by billing you by the hour. The legal system is inherently costly and conflict-ridden. Every dollar you pay your lawyer is a dollar that could have gone to supporting your children.

I've spoken with family lawyers who feel that the system simply chews people up and spits them out, leaving big bills and more anger and toxic emotions behind. The courts view you as a "case," not as a "family." Although you definitely require legal advice, your lawyer can only act upon your direction. You need to be the quarterback who's prepared to call the plays.

Michael Cochrane is a prominent Canadian lawyer and author of numerous books, including *Surviving Your Divorce: A Guide to Canadian Family Law* and *Surviving Your Parents' Divorce: A Guide for Young Canadians.* "We allow people to resolve family law disputes in the same way as we handle breach of contracts," Cochrane explains. "You position yourself, you exchange documents, and the legal pleadings are done in the formula of attack, defend, reply."[19] He believes this allows the court system to further victimize people financially and emotionally.

Cochrane believes a more appropriate model for a divorce would be a labor relations tribunal. "We want people to be able to work together in the long run," he says. "People should get help resolving their dispute, knowing that they have to carry on in the same workplace (or family) and be happy and profitable." Divorce mediators can help divorcing parties create a separation agreement with less stress and cost than duking it out in courts. Cochrane advises caution for people assuming the courts will provide a solution that works for your family and allows you to move forward. "The more dust you kicked up in the divorce, the more you'll have that needs to settle," he warns.

A new brand of family law called the collaborative law process has the potential to change this dynamic. Lawyers represent parties in a collaborative proceeding; however, the lawyers agree that they will work hard to get your case settled so it doesn't have to go to court. If they fail in that, they agree upfront that they will not represent you in any future court proceedings. A collaborative proceeding may also include other specialists to support the process, such as a parenting coordinator, financial professional, or divorce coach. Collaborative law is still in its infancy and has yet to stem the flood of cases going to the courtroom.[20]

Until alternative ways to resolve disputes between warring parents become the rule, rather than the exception, relying solely on the courts and your lawyers to sort out your relationship with your ex isn't a good strategy. The adversarial courtroom environment is inevitably costly and emotionally toxic to cooperative long-term relationships between former spouses. The children will not be immune to the stress and hardship a hard-fought court battle creates. "Unfortunately, quite a few lawyers are a part of the problem. There are lots of really good lawyers who know how to get a case settled," says Cochrane. "It's a big machine. If you only have a hammer, everything starts to look like a nail."

Take Action!

1. Identify the physical and emotional clues you get when you are emotionally "hijacked." Does your face flush? Do you get a lump in your throat? Do you have a negative inner dialogue? Write down the clues so you can become more aware of them.

SIGNS OF AN EMOTIONAL HIJACKING

My physical clues are:

_____

_____

_____

_____

_____

My inner dialogue says:

_____

_____

_____

_____

_____

Take Action!

✔ Accountability Check

☐   I will complete this exercise by: _____

☐   I completed this exercise on: _____

♫ *Remember to Celebrate!* 🎤

2.   Do some preplanning. What are some of the situations that typically get you plugged in to your ex-spouse? Examples might include holidays, times when you transfer the children from one home to the other, or when you have to request a change to the schedule. For each situation, identify one choice you could make to better prepare yourself. You might want to create a script ahead of time of things you could say, or decide to use e-mail to communicate.

ADVANCE PLANNING GUIDE

Situations where I get hooked	Choices I could make instead

Take Action!

 Accountability Check

☐   I will complete this exercise by: _____

☐   I completed this exercise on: _____

♫ *Remember to Celebrate!* ♪

Remember to record your actions in the "Take Action!" Tracker at the end of the book.

CHAPTER SIX

Pitfall #3: Parenting from Guilt

"One doesn't discover new lands without consenting to lose sight of the shore for a very long time."

Andre Gide

When a couple decides to separate and starts the process of splitting up the children's family home into two separated homes, there is inevitably a sense of guilt. Divorce is an adult problem created between two adults, but as parents watching our children adjust to going to "mom's house" and "dad's house" and spending time apart from one of their parents, it can break your heart just a little bit more.

Most parents cannot stand to see their children suffer in any way. We feel the burden and guilt of having created that pain for our children. The dictionary defines guilt as "the remorseful awareness of having done something wrong; self-reproach for supposed inadequacy or wrongdoing." Doesn't just reading that definition make your heart feel heavy?

New York Times best-selling author Debbie Ford shares her story of her own personal sense of guilt when she and her husband separated. "I was the product of a divorce myself, and I felt it had such a negative effect on me. I had an aching in my heart when we separated. My son was only one year old, so I questioned how I could live with myself with this sense of guilt, pain, and shame from choosing to get divorced."[21] Ford's deep anguish and longing for healing led her to write *Spiritual Divorce: Divorce as a Catalyst for an Extraordinary Life*. This book has profoundly changed the lives of hundreds of thousands of people, including mine. I highly recommend her book to you.

Signs That You're Stuck

- **Repetitive negative thoughts**—You cycle through a repeating pattern of thoughts that forecast gloom and doom for your children's emotional well-being. The voice in your head says, "What have I done? My children are never going to be able to get over this divorce!"
- **Frequent pangs of guilt**—Even in the midst of a joyful moment with your children, you experience pangs of guilt or anxiety that life "shouldn't be like this" or "this would be better if we hadn't gotten divorced." Guilt robs you of being present and able to fully enjoy the moment with your children.
- **Assuming the worst**—You conclude your divorce is to blame for common childhood situations, such as your child doing something wrong, acting out, or having a bad day.
- **Beating yourself up**—You spend a lot of time and energy beating yourself up with self-criticism or self-doubt, second-guessing your decisions and instincts.

Guilt Is a Choice

Eleanor Roosevelt once said, "No one can make you feel inferior without your consent." Similarly, no one can make you feel guilty without your consent. If you feel guilty about your divorce and about the impact it has, you are on an unconscious level participating in creating that sense of guilt. If guilt makes us feel bad, why then do we choose to feel guilty?

Many people experience dividends of guilt. What do you get out of feeling guilty? You receive some kind of payback or benefit when you allow yourself to feel guilty, otherwise you wouldn't feel that way.

So take a look and see for yourself. Some people express guilt about the situation as a way to elicit sympathy from others. "Gosh, I feel so bad about Susie and Bill schlepping back and forth between our houses." It's easy to imagine getting a response of, "Oh, don't be so hard on yourself. It's tough, but you're doing the best job you can." Perhaps you want people to assure you that you're going to be better off divorced than you were married.

Sometimes people use guilt as a way to stay stuck and powerless. By expressing guilt that you've doomed your children to grow up in a "broken" family, you have a ready-made excuse when your children misbehave. Perhaps you can get people to join you in bad-mouthing and denigrating your ex-spouse. As the saying goes, misery loves company. But you need to ask yourself—is this the kind of company you want to be keeping?

"I knew that ending my abusive marriage was the best thing for me and my children," said Lynn, a mother of two preschool-age children. "But I felt terribly guilty when the children got upset they weren't going to be seeing their dad every weekend. I second-guess my decision to end the marriage all the time. I question if I did enough to fix our problems."

Wouter van der Hall, creator of *The Parent Program*, says parenting from a sense of guilt is not doing your children any favors. "Your guilt is about you. It has nothing to do with your kids," he argues. "Your children then have to fulfill your need to reduce your sense of guilt. Energy being spent on guilt is not being spent on your kids."[22]

Sometimes guilt can be expressed in ways that don't serve your new lifestyle. "I overextended myself financially on summer vacations the first few years," admitted Marilyn, a mom of three. "I felt we needed that in order to maintain the appearance of being an intact family."

What You See IS What You Get

When parents operate from guilt and blame, problems can arise quite easily. Parents look for what's wrong in their current situation. There is a myth that children will be better and do better if both parents are living under one roof. Isn't that how the picture of a happy family is supposed to look?

If that's not your reality, you may think that getting divorced has condemned your child to living in a "broken" home. Even the word "broken" implies something damaged, irreparable, or defective. If you focus your attention on what's "broken" in your world, you will find lots of examples of how things appear broken or "not right" to you.

What you focus your attention on expands. You may have noticed this when you first got engaged. When you wore an engagement ring, did you suddenly notice how many other people were wearing engagement rings? Or when you were first pregnant, did you notice how many other pregnant people there appeared to be in the world? When you bought the sports car you always wanted, did you notice they seemed to clog the streets? These are some simple examples of how this universal law operates.

There is a huge cost to a child's self-esteem when they feel like they are from a "broken" home. "I feel like I've damaged my kids for life, because my marriage failed," laments Lynn. If you parent believing you've handed your children some kind of a burdensome life sentence, your resilience and resourcefulness as a parent are going to be challenged.

What would be available if you, instead, viewed your divorce as a great learning opportunity for both you and for your children? This change in perspective would change your mind-set and the quality of your divorce experience.

As an example, suppose little Johnny starts to have difficulty in school. Looking through a lens of guilt, shame, or pain, you might conclude, "Johnny is suffering at school because of the divorce." Guilt rises and the hand-wringing and second-guessing begins.

But is that the only possible conclusion? Maybe Johnny needs glasses. Perhaps he's sitting next to someone in class who is disrupting his concentration. If you are so locked into the perspective of guilt, you have only a limited perspective of how to deal with the problems at hand. Just like a horse wearing blinders to keep it on a narrow path, the sense of guilt shields you from seeing any new possibilities, opportunities, or resources that might be available to assist you.

"Doing" instead of "Being"

Parenting from guilt can cause you to focus on "doing" things with your children, as opposed to "being" with them. Take a look at your child's post-divorce schedule to see if this is going on in your household. Often when faced with uncomfortable or unfamiliar feelings of loss, anger, or grief, people distract themselves with activities and work. The result is children who could use a personal assistant to keep track of their after-school and weekend activities! They have little downtime to rest, play, or let their imaginations create new games or adventures. With all of this excessive external stimulation, we raise our children to have less inner resilience and resourcefulness than they might otherwise have.

The "Disneyland Dad" phenomenon is a result of falling into the "parenting from guilt" pitfall. Dads are not the only ones guilty of going overboard on activities. The parent without primary custody may feel an even greater sense of loss or estrangement from his or her child and want to "make up for lost time" as a result. "When my children come back from their dad's on Sunday night, they're exhausted!" complains Suzanne, the mother of ten-year-old twins. "They've seen two theater movies, visited the zoo, watched four videos, and gone to a baseball game, all in one weekend! No kidding there's no time to get their homework done. Then I get to be the bad guy and make sure they're ready for school Monday morning!"

With relatively little time with their children, the noncustodial parent can be consumed with guilt and want to make sure that what little time they have together is all positive. The "Disneyland Dad" may also take the children on expensive vacations or offer them experiences that are out of the usual range of what the children had when the marriage was intact. Discipline on basic child-rearing, such as bedtimes, chores, and good manners, can fall by the wayside to keep everybody happy. The cost is that children start to equate being loved with the presence of special gifts, unique experiences, fewer rules, or over-the-top vacations.

Getting Rid of Guilt

Parenting from a perspective of guilt is somewhat like driving your car by looking through the rear-view mirror. Occasionally you'll see something helpful, but you're missing so much of what's right in front of you. To get rid of guilt, the following strategies should help:

1. Be aware of any active guilt complexes.
2. Choose "being" instead of "buying" with your children.
3. Question yourself and choose thoughts that move you forward, not backward.

1.   Be Aware of Your Guilt Complexes

Awareness of your default programming and guilt complexes is the first and most crucial step in turning things around. Awareness is the first crucial step in turning things around. Noticing where your thoughts or actions are motivated by guilt will help you to make different choices. Embracing a THRIVE mindset will help immensely to empower you. Guilt is a choice. Through awareness, you can choose not to parent from guilt.

2.   Choose "Being" Instead of "Buying"

The most important gift you can give your child, whether you are divorced or not, is your love. When divorce creates two separate homes, it gets more challenging to articulate and demonstrate that love on a daily basis simply because you now live for some portion of time under a different roof than your child. When you are with your child they want *you*—your attention, your listening, and your physical presence. It's not possible to spoil a child with too much love.

However, it is possible to spoil your children. Professor Laurence Steinberg, PhD, and author of *The 10 Basic Principles of Good Parenting*, argues that spoiling a child is "usually the consequence of giving a child things **in place of** love—things like leniency, lowered expectations, or material possessions. Children are harmed when their parents don't set limits for them, when parents lower their expectations for them as a way of being nice, or when toys or food or gifts are used to substitute for genuine affection or attention."[23] From his decades of research and practice as a psychologist and a parent, Steinberg concludes that "when children feel genuinely loved, they develop such a strong sense of security that they are almost always less needy."[24]

3.   Question Yourself

If you are plagued from time to time with thoughts of doom and gloom about your children's future or your own, question yourself honestly. Is that really the truth? Or is that just a fear? A great acronym for the word "fear" is "false expectations appearing real." I created the acronym "feeling expansion and resisting." Fear is simply an indication that you are at the edge of your existing comfort zone.

Can you remember a time when your anticipation of an event created fear? Perhaps it was getting a root canal or the prospect of childbirth for the first time. When you went through it, were you surprised and relieved that it wasn't as bad as you thought?

Find a productive way to express those doubts and fears. Journaling or speaking with a trusted friend is a great start. Acknowledge fear as just an indicator you are moving beyond what feels familiar to you and celebrate your growth as a human being.

So I encourage you to set aside any guilt you may suffer from and deal with your situation in the present moment. The following action items can get you started today.

Take Action!

1. Consider the following questions and spend five to ten minutes writing down your answers:
    *   What kind of lens do you use in viewing your life? Do you view life from a perspective of guilt? Do you view life from a perspective of opportunity for growth and learning?
    *   If you have moments of guilt, notice the inner dialogue you hear. Write what your dialogue sounds like.

BUILDING MY AWARENESS OF GUILT

The lens I typically use is:

_____

_____

_____

_____

_____

_____

_____

_____

_____

_____

_____

_____

Take Action!

My inner dialogue of guilt says:

_____

_____

_____

_____

_____

_____

_____

_____

_____

_____

_____

_____

_____

✔ Accountability Check

☐ I will complete this exercise by: _____

☐ I completed this exercise on: _____

♫ *Remember to Celebrate!* ♪

Take Action!

2.   What are five lessons you can learn from your divorce? For example, "I can learn to be self-reliant." Write down the lessons you can learn.

LESSONS I CAN LEARN FROM MY DIVORCE

Lesson 1:_____

_____

_____

Lesson 2:_____

_____

_____

Lesson 3:_____

_____

_____

Lesson 4:_____

_____

_____

Lesson 5:_____

_____

_____

Take Action!

✔ ## Accountability Check

☐ I will complete this exercise by: _____

☐ I completed this exercise on: _____

♫ *Remember to Celebrate!* ♪

3. What are five lessons your children can learn from your divorce? For example, "My children can learn to be flexible" or "My children can create their own relationship with their other parent." Write down these lessons.

LESSONS MY CHILDREN CAN LEARN FROM MY DIVORCE

Lesson 1:_____

_____

_____

Lesson 2:_____

_____

_____

Take Action!

Lesson 3:_____

_____

_____

Lesson 4:_____

_____

_____

Lesson 5:_____

_____

_____

✔ Accountability Check

☐   I will complete this exercise by: _____

☐   I completed this exercise on: _____

♪ *Remember to Celebrate!* 🎤

Remember to record your actions in the "Take Action!" Tracker at the end of the book.

CHAPTER SEVEN

Pitfall #4: Going for the Martyr Medal

"Why not go out on a limb? Isn't that where the fruit is?"

Mark Twain

Divorce is one of the most emotionally demanding life transitions you'll ever encounter. One big pitfall is getting preoccupied and consumed with making sure everyone else is taken care of first. Single parents easily let their own needs fall by the wayside.

Signs That You're Stuck

- **Having difficulty delegating.** You find it hard to ask for help or delegate everyday chores to others, including your children.
- **Keeping a stiff upper lip.** You feel you must keep up a strong, brave front at all costs and at all times for the sake of your children, even if you're feeling emotionally overwhelmed or unsettled. The thought

of sharing your true feelings with your children feels irresponsible or scary to you.

- **Feeling unappreciated.** You generally feel that people take you for granted. You think that if you do it all yourself and don't complain, one day somebody will notice your efforts and thank you.

The Stress of Divorce

Divorce definitely is a major cause of stress. Becoming divorced rips through the entire fabric of your life. It affects you not only emotionally, but financially, socially, and in some cases, professionally and geographically as well.

The Social Readjustment Rating Scale, developed by Miller and Rahe, ranks various life changes with a point scale according to level of stress. A score below 125 means you're at low risk of stress. A score above 300 puts you at a high risk of stress and potential illness. Just take a look at some of the stress factors that can be involved in a typical divorce:

Example of Factors in a Typical Divorce[25]

Life Events	Stress Points
Divorce	96
Major change in living conditions	42
Change in family get-togethers	25
Major change in health or behavior of family members	55
Major decision about immediate future	51
Decreased income	60
Major change in sleeping habits	26
Major change in usual and/or amount of recreation	28
TOTAL STRESS POINTS	**383**

In this example, this "typical" divorce easily racked up 383 points. That's well over the 300 threshold points considered to put you at risk of stress-related illness! I share this not to scare you, but just to put into perspective what a huge impact divorce can have and how important it is for you to get the resources and the support you need to cope with this upheaval. For people who face threats to their physical safety, this support might include help from lawyers, the courts, and the police.

The Costs of Martyrdom

Some single parents adopt a martyr role as they navigate the new waters of their life. "Yes, my life is tough right now but I'll just soldier on, even if I'm miserable and not getting enough sleep." Self-care may seem like a theoretical luxury—after all, who's got the time when you're dealing with a maelstrom of issues that demand your attention as a newly divorced parent? Why, you've got to handle the kids, the ex, the finances, the lawyers, setting up mom's house and dad's house, the family repercussions of your split, and the impact of your divorce on your friends and social network. You can feel like you don't have time to breathe, let alone deal with any anger or grief you're feeling because a major relationship has ended.

If you are trying to capture a medal for being a self-sacrificing martyr, I have some news for you. There are no medals for martyrs. The International Olympic Committee is not adding it to their event list anytime soon. Nobody, particularly not your children, will come to you at some point in the future and say, "I appreciate how much you sacrificed your own health and well-being for us—and how you let us know about it all along the way!" Divorce summons all of your internal resources, and at this point in time, your commitment to self-care will never be more tested or more needed.

Single parenting requires a lot from you. It's hard to meet the challenges when your inner resources and resilience are low. When emotions are high, intelligence seems to drop proportionally. One consequence of parenting from this diminished state is that your fuse gets short. Have you noticed that? One small thing doesn't go according to plan, one child decides she doesn't want to eat breakfast, and then WHAM! The fuse lights the powder keg inside of you and you are hijacked by an emotional outburst that's completely out of proportion to the incident that sparked the explosion. "I felt so guilty afterwards," confessed John. "My six-year-old son didn't want to put on his socks in the morning, and next thing I know, I'm bellowing at him like he's set the house on fire. It broke my heart to see the way he looked at me."

"The biggest challenge I faced when I first separated was anger with my children," confessed Marie. "I was trying to heal myself and deal with exactly the same issues that stemmed in my childhood while taking care of my two children. It was overwhelming. I wasn't sure how to take care of me, let alone be the mom who takes care of the kids." Marie's story is typical of many single parents. Luckily, Marie had a great teacher in the form of her son. "I was telling my nine-year-old son, Michael, one day that he could do anything he wants to do. He looked at me and said, 'Mom, don't you know the same is true for you?' That woke me up! It was then that I realized how right he was and how necessary it was for me to pay attention to my own needs too, and not just the children's needs."

On the one hand, it's difficult to parent your children single-handedly. On the other hand, when your children leave to visit their other parent, you're left with an unexpected void or emptiness in your life. Perhaps you even feel a bit of guilty pleasure to have your own home all to yourself for a few hours or a weekend without your children.

Think about the safety announcements you hear in airplanes, advising adults to put the oxygen masks on themselves first and then assist their children. If you have passed out from lack of oxygen at 30,000 feet, what good will you be to your children in that state? The same principle applies in divorce. You must be aware of your own needs and take responsibility for taking care of yourself. Your commitment to self-care is one of the most important gifts you can give yourself—and your children.

Strategies for Single-Parent Self-Care

When single parents let their own reserves get low, they are more likely to leak emotional toxins all over their children. Take a moment to imagine the innocent heart of your child as if it were a sponge. In the early emotional stages of development, a child's heart is incredibly absorbent and soaks in every tone, raised eyebrow, or raised voice. How would you treat your children when they're down, exhausted, or scared? Would you tell them, "Get your act together and stop whining!" or "It sounds like you've had a hard day. What would make you feel better?" Treat yourself with the same love and care you give your children.

Taking care of yourself is imperative. The following strategies can get the ball rolling:

1. Give yourself five minutes a day.
2. Find emotional support.

3. Delegate as much as possible.
4. Appreciate yourself.
5. Be a role model for your children.

1. Give Yourself Five Minutes a Day

Self-care doesn't have to be big, fancy, expensive, or time consuming. Being a parent is just one of the many roles we play. We are also sisters, daughters, brothers, sons, friends, colleagues, community members, business people, artists, and seekers. Wouter van der Hall, founder of *The Parent Program*, recommends that all parents take at least five uninterrupted minutes each day to give to themselves, even if it's just to read, do some conscious breathing, draw a sketch, or call a friend. "Kids want to see you as more than just a parent," van der Hall advises. "They want to see you reach your own goals. Taking care of yourself gives them an example to follow. You'll become less resentful about all the time you put into your children and your divorce situation."

Surely you are deserving of at least five minutes of your undivided attention each day. Let that be your first step.

2. Find Emotional Support

Ending a marriage touches almost every part of your life—your emotional world, your finances, your family, your social structure of family and friends, and your shelter. Moving through divorce is like peeling an onion. Just when you think you've finished and are "over it," often something happens that sets you back emotionally and lets you see there's yet another layer for you to process. It may be remembering your wedding anniversary, learning your ex-spouse is in a new relationship, having your child ask you a question about why Mommy and Daddy don't live together anymore, or even going on your first date after your separation.

You need to find appropriate emotional support as you go on this journey. It may be some close friends who are also single parents, or you may want to work with a therapist, divorce coach, counselor, or social worker for a time. Visit www.ThriveAfterDivorce.com for resources such as divorce coaching. You can check your local Yellow Pages or neighborhood newsletters for listings of agencies or support groups in your area for single parents. There are a growing number of online divorce support resources as well. Social service agencies offer educational programs or seminars that can be informative not only for you, but for your former partner and children as well. Many employers have an employee assistance program that can offer you counseling. It's important that you put a structure together to help support you and guide you through this life transition.

3. Delegate as much as Possible

Are there any responsibilities that you have now that you may need to delegate or defer to give yourself some time off? Add names to your babysitter list or consider doing a child-care swap. Make agreements with your employer or co-workers to pitch in if you need to get the children from school. Hire neighborhood kids to help with yard work or snow shoveling. Keep a list of reliable tradespeople handy so next time the sink is backed up or the fridge goes on the fritz, you have someone you trust to call.

4. Appreciate Yourself

A big reason people become self-sacrificing martyrs is because they are really seeking acknowledgement and appreciation. Unconsciously, they are trying to fill a void inside themselves that craves attention and acknowledgement, so by "doing it all" martyrs hope that someday someone will come to them and say, "Thanks for the great job you're doing!"

There is a much more reliable and dependable way to receive that acknowledgement that is available to you 24/7: **Acknowledge yourself.** Acknowledgment is a healing balm to our soul, letting us know that we are doing the best we can with the tools we have. If we never stop to appreciate ourselves, we open up a hole in our hearts, which craves recognition. This is one reason why celebrating successes is so important and was introduced at the beginning of the book as part of your action and accountability check.

Some of us are minimizers, downplaying our accomplishments or being critical because we made a mistake or didn't do something perfectly. Since when did we expect ourselves, flawed and imperfect human beings that we are, to never make a mistake? Is that the expectation we hold for our children? Of course not! Part of the beauty and joy we experience in our journey of life is that we are always capable of learning and growing. It's vital that we stop to acknowledge ourselves for who we are and how far we've come.

5. Be A Role Model for Your Children

Have you noticed that children will do what you do, not what you say? What kind of lesson do you want your children to learn if you are perpetually self-sacrificing? Give that some serious thought. The parent going for the martyr medal teaches his or her children to ignore their own needs and sacrifice themselves for others, even to the point of their own detriment. The example the martyr-parent sets for his or her children is that it's acceptable to rely on other people to feed them a sense of self-worth. Is that really what you want for your children?

Instead, how about choosing to be a model of a real and authentic human being? As human beings, we have a huge emotional range that encompasses joy and creativity on one end of the spectrum and overwhelm and anger on the other. You can model to your children how to handle all of their emotions, not just the socially acceptable ones. As one of my mentors, T. Harv Eker, expresses it, emotion is simply energy in motion. Feelings are like waves that pass through us, and it's only when we try to block, ignore, or stuff them that we get stuck.

If you're feeling overwhelmed or scared, you can start by simply naming that feeling. Let your children know "Mommy is feeling overwhelmed right now," or "Daddy is kind of scared." Help your children build their own emotional vocabulary.

The next step is to ask yourself what you need to do in that moment to take care of yourself. You can demonstrate that to your children as well, by saying, "Daddy needs to take a ten-minute break to collect his thoughts," or "Mommy could use a hug from you and then some help getting this kitchen cleaned up." Taking responsibility for your feelings and taking care of yourself is a powerful legacy to leave your children.

Take Action!

1.   What are some of the specific ways that you currently "go for the martyr medal"? List them.

MY "MARTYR MEDAL" EVENTS

The ways I "go for the martyr medal" include:

_____

_____

_____

_____

_____

_____

_____

_____

_____

_____

_____

Take Action!

✔ # Accountability Check

☐ I will complete this exercise by: _____

☐ I completed this exercise on: _____

🎵 *Remember to Celebrate!* 🎤

2. Write your own prescription for the "I wanna be a martyr" syndrome. There are three steps to creating your antidote to this single-parenting pitfall. (To download a worksheet and create your prescription, visit www.7pitfalls.com.)

YOUR PRESCRIPTION FOR "I WANNA BE A MARTYR" SYNDROME

Step 1: Write a list of at least five ways people in your life appreciate you now by completing the following statement.

_____ **appreciate me for** _____.

For example, "*My children* appreciate me for *being such a fun mother*."

_____ **appreciate me for** _____.

_____ **appreciate me for** _____.

_____ **appreciate me for** _____.

_____ **appreciate me for** _____.

_____ **appreciate me for** _____.

Take Action!

Step 2: After you've completed the sentence at least five times, use your answers to create your own personalized prescription. Review your list and complete the following statement.

I appreciate and acknowledge myself for _____.

Starting with the first item, complete the blank with the same *information* you completed in Step 1.
For example, "I appreciate and acknowledge myself for <u>being such a fun mother</u>."

Repeat this process for each statement you created in Step 1.

I appreciate and acknowledge myself for _____.

I appreciate and acknowledge myself for _____.

I appreciate and acknowledge myself for _____.

I appreciate and acknowledge myself for _____.

I appreciate and acknowledge myself for _____.

Step 3: Write out the statements you created in Step 2 on a fresh sheet of paper or an index card. Review and repeat this prescription out loud to yourself for the next twenty-one days.

✔ Accountability Check

☐   I will complete this exercise by: _____

☐   I completed this exercise on: _____

♫ *Remember to Celebrate!* ♪

Take Action!

3. Play the Appreciation Game with your children. Bedtime is a great time to play this game. While saying goodnight to your child, ask your child to identify at least two things they were proud of themselves for or that they felt happy about from the day. Acknowledge your child's answers with a "Good job!" or a big hug. Then you take a turn, sharing what you would like to acknowledge yourself for from your day. It's a wonderful way to connect with your child! Commit to playing the Appreciation Game at least twice in the next week.

✔ ## Accountability Check

☐   I will complete this exercise by: _____

☐   I completed this exercise on: _____

♫ *Remember to Celebrate!* ♪

Remember to record your actions in the "Take Action!" Tracker at the end of the book.

CHAPTER EIGHT

Pitfall #5: Not Putting Your Children First

"Courage is not the absence of fear, but rather the judgment that something else is more important than fear."

Ambrose Redmoon

It is so important to put the best interests of your children first at all times. Divorce occurs between two adults and stems from issues that arose between you and your former spouse. The children you had together are the innocent bystanders to your relationship breakdown. Children are young, vulnerable, and incredibly intuitive. How you parent them, postdivorce, will have a significant impact on whether they will flourish after divorce or end up as collateral damage. Your children will use what they experience of their own parents' relationship as a model for how they'll select their partners and create their relationships.

Signs That You're Stuck

- **Being openly critical of your ex to your children**—You express your own anger, frustration, and criticism of your former partner to your children. When your children bring up a concern about their other parent, you can't resist making a sarcastic or disparaging comment about the parent. You'll criticize or gossip about your former partner with your friends or family, even if your children are within earshot. You feel it's important to share your truth with your children about what you see as the real character of their other parent.

- **Using your children as messengers or spies**—You ask your children to convey messages from you to their other parent for two reasons. First, you feel unable to communicate directly with your ex for whatever reasons. Second, you think your chances of receiving a positive answer to your requests will be higher if the children are the ones carrying the request. You ask your children intrusive questions about your ex's life. You rationalize turning your children into spies because you feel you need to keep tabs on your ex for the sake of your children.

- **Depending on your children as a shoulder to cry on**—You allow your children to become your confidants and friends by sharing some of your intimate, emotional fears and personal issues with them. You believe this brings you closer to your children, and they seem to be able to handle it, so you don't believe there's any harm in this.

- **Using your children as bargaining chips**—If your ex doesn't meet his or her agreements in any way, such as child support, schedules, or parenting styles, you threaten to withhold access to the children until your ex toes the line you set.

- **Your way or the highway**—You are unwilling to be flexible. When your ex requests changes to the children's schedule to accommodate something out of the ordinary, your allegiance is first and foremost to the schedule and whether it's convenient to you. You rarely ask yourself if saying yes to the requested change would be in your children's best interests.

Bad-mouthing or Blaming Your Ex-Spouse to Your Children

It may seem obvious to say it, but sadly many single parents continually bad-mouth the other parent because they are so caught in their own emotional pain after separation. For example, "Your dad's late because he's selfish and doesn't care about us!" or "Mom is just being mean because she is jealous of Daddy's new lady friend." Bad-mouthing your ex-partner is incredibly toxic to the child, who feels stuck in between the two people your child loves the most.

Sometimes the bad-mouthing isn't done directly in front of the child. Disparaging your ex on the phone or over coffee with a friend, with your child in potential earshot, is not advisable. "My six-year-old daughter said to me out of the blue the other day that 'All men are irresponsible,'" said Marina. "She could barely say the word 'irresponsible,' and I knew that she must have picked that up somehow from me. That's when I realized that my daughter likes to play computer games when I'm on the phone to my friends. She must have overheard me talking." In this case, Marina's daughter is simply parroting back what she's heard, likely in an attempt to demonstrate her love for her mom and her desire to comfort her mother during a time of transition.

Sometimes demeaning your ex in front of your children isn't always verbal. Be alert for nonverbal ways that you signal your frustration or lack of respect for your former spouse. Rolling your eyes, taking some deep sighs while you hear about what's going on at the other parent's home, putting your hands on your hips, or crossing your arms when you discuss the other parent are common. These nonverbal cues say, "I don't like this" or "I'm skeptical" or "I'm right, and she's wrong." Remember, children are very intuitive, and they pick up those signals even on a subconscious level.

Making children choose a side between Mom and Dad is unhealthy for their long-term happiness and success. As one single parent stated it, "When you make your child choose in any way, they don't feel free to love either parent. It's kind of like adding rat poison to their breakfast cereal!"

Parents who demean the other parent to their children typically do it to foster a greater sense of loyalty to them. This strategy can backfire in the long run. According to Dr. Joan Kelly, research shows that young adults of college age are "more angry at parents who interfered with contacts or demeaned the other parent."[26]

In some cases, bad-mouthing may escalate to outright brainwashing or even "parental alienation syndrome," a term coined by Dr. Richard Gardner to describe the situation in which a child completely rejects a relationship with one parent. In his book *Divorce Poison*, Dr. Richard Warshak offers five excellent self-assessment questions to use before commenting to children about their other parent. While lapses in judgment at times are to be expected, the questions "will help you cut through self-deception, expose irrational motives that could be fueling your behavior, and focus attention on your children's genuine welfare."[27] According to Dr. Warshak, the questions to consider **before** you reveal something to your children about their other parent are:

- What is the real reason for revealing this information to my children?
- Are my children being harmed by the behavior I am about to criticize? Or are they being harmed by not having the information I am about to reveal?
- How will it help the children to hear what I am about to tell them?
- Do the possible benefits of revealing this to the children outweigh the possible risks?
- If I were still happily married to my spouse, and I wanted to protect our children's relationship with him or her, how would I handle the situation?

Children as Messengers and Spies

Too often, children get caught in the crossfire of the divorce game their parents play. It's a big mistake to put your child in the role of messenger for communications that should take place between you and your ex. "Initially, I did ask my nine-year-old son to convey information to his father for me," confessed Sandra. "I rationalized it because I was so steamed at his dad I was worried I'd say something I might later regret. Looking back on it now, I see what a burden I had put on his young shoulders. For Tim to be put in the position of telling his dad when he had to be back at my house, or that he wasn't allowed to play on his computer after dinner at my house, simply wasn't fair. No wonder Tim started to get very quiet and withdrawn. His dad was angry at me and ended up taking it out on the messenger."

Asking your children questions about what your ex-partner is up to in a detailed, intrusive way is also not appropriate. Let your children share without you actively digging for gossip about whether Daddy has a girlfriend or how Mommy is spending her money. Fishing for information about your former partner not only puts your children in the middle, but it may cause them to start to hide information from you.

Children need to be children. They understand instinctively they are the product of two people—Mom and Dad. The natural tendency for children is to take any upset or disruption personally. "If Mom and Daddy can't get along, it must be because of something I did" is a common conclusion. Putting your child in the role of messenger or spy between two disputing adults is not only ineffective, but it's unfair to your child.

Family lawyer Michael Cochrane tells of a case where a mother took her eight-year-old child through a legal document written by a caseworker involved in her custody dispute. "This woman had a completely misplaced sense of protecting her child's best interest," Cochrane observes. "She was really protecting her own personal interests."[28] Not only does it create tension and stress for your child, but it sets your child up to have divided loyalties or desires to play peacemaker between the two people he or she loves the most.

"When parents focus on raising their children, rather than using them, it helps the children to accept the situation of divorce more easily," advises Wouter van der Hall, creator of *The Parent Program*. "The other parent of your children deserves respect just for that fact. Single parents need to separate out kids' issues from what are parent or adult issues. Your primary role is to make choices that are in the best interests of your children."

Let's take a hypothetical example where Wendy notices that her ex-husband, Phil, is using their eight-year-old son, John, to request a change for the date of his son's next overnight visit to accommodate a family celebration Phil is having.

Wendy:	Did you have a good time at your Dad's this weekend?
John:	Yup. Oh, by the way, Dad wants me to be with him again next weekend. Aunt Carol is coming into town for a visit. That's OK, isn't it?
Wendy:	What! Your Dad wants to have you two weekends in a row and hasn't even asked me?
John:	Gee, Mom, I don't know. I really like Aunt Carol, and that's just what he told me to tell you.
Wendy:	Well, I'm going to tell your dad a few things myself. This is so typical of him to change our agreements without even giving it a second thought! I'm sorry, John, but you're not going if this is how your dad is going to be.
John:	(crying now) I'm sorry, Mom, I didn't mean to get you upset. It's just that I don't see Aunt Carol that much, and I thought it would be OK.

Wendy then gets on the phone with her ex-husband to complain and is unwilling to hear his request. The conversation ends when she hangs up on him.

Here's another way the conversation could go if Wendy were willing to take a stand to not have her son used as a messenger.

Wendy: Did you have a good time at your Dad's this weekend?

John: Yup. Oh, by the way, Dad wants me to be with him again next weekend. Aunt Carol is coming into town for a visit. That's OK, isn't it?

Wendy: Well, John, to be honest, I'm not sure. Making a change in our schedule is something Mom and Dad have to talk about together. I'll get back to you when I've had a chance to speak to him.

John: OK, Mom. Let me know then.

Wendy then goes to call Phil.

Wendy: Hi, Phil! I understand from John that you'd like to have him again next weekend because your sister is coming into town. Is that right?

Phil: Yes. It's important that he be able to spend time with my family, so I told him about it. Is that OK with you?

Wendy: Phil, before I even check my schedule, I request that you speak with me or e-mail me directly about any changes in our children's schedules. I ask you to communicate with me before you tell John and get his hopes up for something that may not happen. By asking John to carry your message, you've put him in the middle of us, and that's not fair.

Phil: C'mon, you don't have to make such a big deal about it. He's a big boy now, and he can do that.

Wendy: I agree he's growing up. Regardless, he is still our son, and it's not fair that he becomes the messenger or mediator between us. Schedules can be contentious. I think we owe it to John to sort out any requests and possible conflicts between ourselves. That way, John won't be disappointed or feel stuck in the middle. I also want to let you know that I won't consider any schedule changes unless you've communicated them to me directly. How would you handle it if our situations were reversed?

Phil: Well, now that you put it that way, I guess I see what you're talking about. OK, I'll talk to you first before I make any promises to John. I won't use him as a shortcut to speaking to you.

Wendy: Thank you. I will make that same commitment to you. I'll take a look at that weekend to see if John can join you for the visit with Aunt Carol, and call you back. I would expect you to be willing to do a similar swap with me in the future if I requested it from you. Can we agree on that?

Phil: Sure thing. Get back to me when you can.

You can empower your children by telling them they do not need to be the messenger of adult communications and that they can ask that the other parent not put them in that position. It's important you do this in a way that does not blame or criticize the other parent. For example, "Sandy, I notice you've been giving me Daddy's messages lately. I think it would be easier on everyone if Daddy and I spoke with each other about those kinds of issues. I've asked Daddy to speak with me, but if he forgets, you can remind him that you don't have to be the messenger anymore."

In most cases, it's in your children's best interest to have a relationship with both parents. The exception to this principle would be cases where you fear the safety or physical well-being of your children or yourself, in which case you should contact the appropriate professionals to keep you safe.

Children as Friends or Confidants

Some single parents mistakenly use their children as confidants. Children love you and will intuitively try to support you and try to "kiss it and make it better." It's important to remember your primary role is to parent your children and allow them to have their own emotional experiences. Children need parents, and that must remain your primary role. If you need a confidant, it's more appropriate to find an adult friend or counselor to listen to you, not your children.

"Growing up I felt it was my job to make sure my mom was happy. She would tell me all about the troubles and resentments she had with my dad while they were still married. It felt weird to hear all that stuff about my dad when I was so young, but I felt like a great daughter because my mom trusted me with that information," said Margaret, whose parents divorced when she was in her late teens. "It was only when I was starting a family of my own that I started to realize how our little 'girl talks' caused me to drift away from my dad."

Trudy is a separated mom with three children, two of whom are in their late teens. When her teenaged daughter pushed for answers to her questions about why Trudy and her ex-husband split up, Trudy crossed a line in what she shared. "I regret the amount I shared with my nineteen-year-old daughter. I ended up concluding a conversation with her with 'Your dad is a fabulous dad, but not such a fabulous husband to me,'" Trudy shares. "Since then, my daughter has been hypersensitive about her father and construes anything I say about him as critical. I should just never have gone there with her." This is a clear example of how children perceive themselves as products of both Mom and Dad and can feel divided loyalties, no matter what age the child is.

Children As Bargaining Chips

It's clearly not in the best interest of your children to use them as pawns or bargaining chips if you and your spouse have a disagreement. Many single parents have withdrawn access to the children as a weapon against their former spouse. Of course you may be aggravated if your ex makes late child-support payments or breaks the child-sharing arrangements in some way. But when you yank access to the children to try to force compliance, you cause pain and confusion to your children.

"My brother was getting married on a weekend when I was scheduled to have the children. The hitch was he was getting married in Italy, and I wanted to take them out of school for a few extra days to allow for travel to Europe," complained Roger. "At first their mother refused to let me take them out of the country at all. Ultimately, my children were able to attend, but it took about six months of arguing, a few hefty lawyer bills, and a couple of rounds of tears from my disappointed children until their mother agreed to let me have them for four days. She was more interested in pursuing her personal vendetta with me than in seeing her children be a part of an important family event."

Don't use your children as bargaining chips. Engage with your ex directly, hire a mediator or lawyer if you need to, but keep your children off the battlefield.

Keeping Your Eyes on the Prize: Your Children

If your children are in a squeeze play between their parents, it's time to stop. Here are some strategies to climb out of this pitfall:
1.   Use your children's best interests as your yardstick.
2.   Create a safe, loving environment.
3.   Develop bench strength.

1. Use Your Children's Best Interests as Your Yardstick

In each decision you make as a coparent, develop the habit of asking yourself, "What would serve my children best in this situation?" Of course, children need structure, and a good parenting plan and separation agreement can provide that. But inevitably, issues will come up that will require you to make a decision. How will you handle it when an important but last-minute family event gets scheduled while the children are with the other parent? What will you do when one parent has to travel and needs flexibility and child-care coverage from the other parent?

If you can be flexible and cooperative with your ex, why not do it if it's in the best interests of your children? These are important ingredients in any successful working partnership, which is what you want to create if your children are going to thrive after divorce.

2. Create a Safe, Loving Environment

During separation, children will go through an emotional roller-coaster, similar to the one you experience. One minute they're happy and outgoing; the next, they may be angry, sad, fearful, or withdrawn. In divorce, children have their own emotional issues to process, which is challenging enough without asking them to take on your issues as well. Children need to learn that they are not responsible for their parents' feelings or emotional well-being. You, as the parent, need to establish where those healthy boundaries are. Children must be encouraged to express their feelings and know they are entitled to their emotions.

It's also important for you to honestly acknowledge your feelings to your children (remember Pitfall #4, "Going for the Martyr Medal"). "Daddy's feeling angry right now, so I just need a few minutes to myself" shows the child the important lessons of identifying and honoring your feelings and the willingness to take care of your emotional needs.

Let them know they are not responsible for fixing you, but that by being able to share how you're feeling, you'll be able to feel better sooner. You also let your children know that you love them unconditionally, regardless of how they are feeling.

You can reflect their feelings back to them as a way of validating them. "You sound really sad right now. I can understand that because there's been a lot of change going on for us as a family right now," would be an appropriate response.

Children need their freedom to be children. Support them by giving them a safe environment to be heard and to express themselves. Create some boundaries for yourself, such as speaking to your ex yourself if you need to address a problem.

3. Develop Bench Strength

The most successful teams have a strong starting line-up and a strong, reliable bench of players ready to be called to action at a moment's notice. That's what you should strive to develop. In our modern society, children seem to grow up so fast already. Asking your child to be your advisor robs them of the freedom to fully enjoy their childhood and creates divided loyalties for them. There are other people who are available to you to be your friend, confidant, coach, therapist, and supporter, seek out another adult to support you.

Take Action!

1. Look back and see if you can identify any examples where you used your children as messengers or bargaining chips. How could you handle that situation more effectively in the future and keep your children's best interest first?

EYES ON THE PRIZE

Examples Where I Haven't Put my Children First	What I Could Do Differently

✔ Accountability Check

☐   I will complete this exercise by: _____

☐   I completed this exercise on: _____

♫ *Remember to Celebrate!* 🎤

Take Action!

2. Create a brief written definition of what you consider to be in your children's best interest. Imagine sharing it with your children. Would they agree with you? If not, where do your views and your children's likely views differ? Consider issues such as your children's freedom to be children, your child being able to love both parents, and your child not having to choose one parent over another.

DEFINING MY CHILDREN'S BEST INTERESTS

I define my children's best interests as including the following characteristics:

_____

_____

_____

_____

_____

_____

_____

_____

_____

_____

_____

_____

_____

Take Action!

✔ Accountability Check

☐   I will complete this exercise by: _____

☐   I completed this exercise on: _____

♪ *Remember to Celebrate!* ♪

Remember to record your actions in the "Take Action!" Tracker at the end of the book.

CHAPTER NINE

Pitfall #6: Being Responsible for Your Children's Relationship with Your Ex

"I hear and I forget. I see and I remember. I do and I understand."

Chinese proverb

Are you responsible for the relationship your children has with their other parent? When you were married, did you find yourself acting as a facilitator or mediator of how your child interacted with or felt around your partner? Did you make it your job to make sure your child loved and respected the other parent? If you saw that your former spouse wasn't listening to your child or taking care of the child the way you thought he or she "should," did you try to "fix it"? If you continue this mediator role when you're separated, it's an invitation to problems.

Signs That You're Stuck

- **You act as a middleman between your children and their other parent.** You love your children so much you'll do anything you can to ensure they never feel unhappy, disappointed, or confused. You believe your job is to act as a middleman or agent for your children, shielding them from having their feelings hurt or being disappointed by their other parent.
- **You try to manage how your ex-spouse parents your children.** Even though your children have two different homes, you feel it's imperative that each household have the same parenting style, the same rules, and the same values. You get upset and vocal when you learn your ex-partner handles situations differently than you would.
- **You enjoy when your children turn to you about issues they have with their other parent.** Your children have become accustomed to sharing their innermost feelings about their other parent with you. You don't encourage your children to share their feelings with their other parent directly. You worry your children will need you less and you won't feel as close to them if they become more independent and voice their issues to the other parent directly.

Two Households, Two Parenting Styles

When married or living together, parents typically assume a "united front" in parenting to provide consistency and clarity for the children. Perhaps you had very different parenting styles when you were together. It may have been quite natural for you to facilitate the relationship your child has with the other parent. Now that you have "Mom's house" and "Dad's house," the differences between how you and your ex relate to your children and parent them will be magnified.

No matter how much you try to be on the same page in terms of discipline, basic rules, chores, and activities, the differences in parenting styles will become quickly apparent. For the sake of your children, you must learn to distinguish what you have responsibility and control over and what you don't. Recall the THRIVE Principle of Responsibility. You are responsible for the rules and code of conduct you have in your household. You are responsible for your thoughts, words, and actions. You may not like it but you have no control or responsibility for the rules, code of conduct, and behavior of your ex-spouse.

"When we were together, we agreed that the children should not watch TV or play computer during the school week," complained Laura. "Now it seems when they're at their dad's house, they do nothing but play video games and watch movies, even if there's homework to do!" Laura admitted she would voice her frustration to her children by making sarcastic comments about her children's father. She also increased her vigilance while the children were with her to make sure homework was completed. The result was more tension and conflict in her relationship with her children.

So what can you do when you find out that your ex has different rules, and you don't necessarily agree with them? Clearly, if you learn that some potentially harmful behavior is going on in the other parent's house, you must address it with your former spouse to keep your children safe. Examples here would include leaving underage children at home unsupervised, not using the proper safety devices in a car, or allowing the children to play with matches.

However, what can Laura, who is concerned about children not getting their homework done, do? If the children's grades begin to slip, the teacher will likely express her concerns. Laura can share the feedback with her ex and request that he ensure that the children do their homework while at his house. Laura can ask the teacher to give that feedback directly to the children's father as well as to her.

One important lesson Laura can share with her children is they are responsible for getting their homework done, regardless of whether they are at her house or their dad's house. If homework isn't completed, the children will face consequences, such as staying in at recess or after school, serving detentions, and falling behind in their work. Instead of being sarcastic with her ex and taking on the mantle of a martyr, Laura can use these action steps to focus on the facts of the situation and create a more productive result.

The other parent will always be your child's parent. Your child and former spouse will always have a relationship, and you need to respect that.

Playing Monkey in the Middle

A mother or a father instinctively looks out for the best interest of the child and wants to protect him or her from any possible harm, danger, or heartache. When you were together with your spouse, it was probably very easy and natural to act as a facilitator or spokesperson for the other parent. Letting yourself be the middleman between your children and their other parent is actually a way to disempower your own children.

Let's take a look at a typical scenario.

Sarah:	"Mom, Daddy doesn't play with me the way that you play with me. It's not as fun at his house as it is here."
Mom:	"Gee, I'm sorry you feel that way. I'm sure Daddy tries to make sure you have fun at his house."
Sarah:	"Yes, but he's always so busy with his work on his computer and on his phone calls. It sucks! I don't think Daddy cares about me."
Mom:	"Well, I'm sure Daddy loves you in his own way. He can get busy at work sometimes, and his work is important." (Or, if Mom is feeling somewhat vindictive she may say, "Well, that's just typical of your father—always putting his work ahead of his family!") "Just try and have fun anyway, if you can. You can always come and talk to me if you're feeling sad."

In this scenario, Mom minimizes Sarah's feelings. Instead of offering possible solutions to her daughter, all she can offer are possible excuses for the behavior of her former spouse. Mom plays "monkey in the middle" by promising her daughter can complain to her in the future. Mom may use this incident as one more piece of evidence she's a better parent than her ex and feel some sense of victory as a result. Sarah is disempowered because she is not shown how she can be a part of the solution to the problem she is experiencing.

Here's how the same scenario could play out if Mom stopped being responsible for her daughter's relationship with her ex-spouse.

Sarah:	"Mom, Daddy doesn't play with me the way that you play with me. It's not as fun at his house as it is here."
Mom:	"Are you saying that you'd like to have more fun with your dad when you're at his house?"
Sarah:	"Yeah, I guess that's what I'm saying."
Mom:	"How do you feel that you're not having fun with him the way you'd like to?"
Sarah:	"Well, I feel kind of sad about it."
Mom:	"So you feel kind of sad about it then. Do you have some ideas of how you could have fun with your dad?"
Sarah:	Yes! I'd love to have him help me build that model airplane I got or play ball at the schoolyard with me.
Mom:	"Great! Sounds like you've got some clear ideas about what would be fun for you and your dad to do together."
Sarah:	"Yeah, I guess I do!"

Mom:	"I've got an idea! Why don't you speak talk to your dad and let him know how you've been feeling about this, and propose some of your ideas to him yourself?"
Sarah:	"I don't know. What if he says no?"
Mom:	"You'll never know unless you try. Your job is to let your dad know what's going on with you. If you don't talk to him, how will he know what you need unless he's turned into a mind reader? Would you be willing to try?"
Sarah:	"OK, I'll talk to Dad. Thanks, Mom!"

In this scenario, Sarah feels heard, and her feelings are validated. Most importantly, Mom uses questions to help Sarah articulate a solution to her problem, which empowers her. The responsibility for the quality of Sarah's relationship with her father remains with Sarah and has not been assumed by Mom. Sarah has learned she is responsible for voicing her feelings and ideas to her dad directly and asking for what she needs, instead of relying on a third-party (her mom) to satisfy her desires.

The bottom line is your former spouse will always be the parent of your child. What the relationship looks like and feels like for your child is ultimately the responsibility of your child and the other parent, not you. Making yourself responsible for being a shield or facilitator for your child is ultimately a recipe for disaster. You must be willing to let your child create and develop his or her own relationship with the other parent, even if that means some emotional disappointments or upsets for your child in the short term. In the long run, you are supporting your child in being responsible for the quality of his or her relationships.

Clash of Parenting Styles

Parents have different ways they want to raise their children. You may have noticed or even struggled with this reality when you were married. Getting divorced tends to expose more clearly those differences.

Marcella noticed how the difference in parenting styles affected her seven-year-old daughter, Molly. When Molly was with her mom, she accidentally spilled some water and started to get really upset about it. "Daddy gets really mad when I make a mistake and spill things," sobbed Molly. Initially, Marcella became indignant and imagined that her daughter had been ridiculed by her ex for making an innocent mistake. Luckily, Marcella took a deep breath and reframed the situation beautifully for her daughter. "I see that you had an accident, and I know that you'll be able to clean it up, Molly," Marcella explained. "I know I make mistakes, and the neat thing is I learn a lot from my mistakes. Do you want to learn how to clean this mess up with me?"

You can let your children know people have different ways of doing things. Without making the other parent "wrong," you can teach your child that in your house you have certain rules and agreements. In the other parent's house, those rules may be different, and it's up to your child to understand those rules and work with the other parent.

When the Other Parent Is Not Involved with the Children

In some cases, one parent is not actively involved in the lives of the children after the marriage ends. In those cases, the custodial parent needs to make it clear that this choice is not the child's responsibility. Teach your children everyone can make choices and everyone can make mistakes, children and adults alike. If mommy or daddy is not involved, encourage your children to not take it personally or make it "mean" something about them. Give them the ability to create a new conclusion. For example, "Daddy is really angry and needs to take care of himself like this for now," as opposed to "Daddy is really angry, and it must be my fault."

Strategies to Step Out

There are a number of ways you can wean yourself from being responsible for your child's relationship with your former spouse and empower your children at the same time. They are:

1. Be a resource person, not a rescue person.
2. Empower your children.
3. Intervene only when needed.

1. Be a Resource Person, Not a Rescue Person

Imagine the characteristics or life skills you'd like your children to have when they are adults. Would you like them to be loving, responsible, emotionally aware, independent adults? Do you want them to be able to make healthy decisions for themselves? Every choice you make as a parent right now will support your child in being able to develop those life skills or not.

Stepping in to rescue your child from every situation where there is friction between your child and your ex-spouse will not support him or her in developing independence and decision-making skills in the long run. Rescue-parents jump into the fray to do battle on behalf their child. They draw quick conclusions and don't involve their child in problem-solving. The child is relieved of any responsibility or involvement for dealing with his or her problems. The child is insulated and protected from developing a relationship on his own terms with the other parent. This can set up a dynamic where the child grows up looking for more rescuers as he hasn't developed the internal emotional resources or skills to manage their own problems.

Support your children by being a loving resource person instead. Resource-parents acknowledge the child's feelings. Resource-parents engage their children in dialogue about the nature of the problems they face. Resource-parents encourage their children to actively brainstorm possible solutions. The resource-parent is a facilitator for problem solving and offers unconditional support. A resource-parent is not a knight on a white horse. The child is given a clear role and responsibility in solving their own problem. The child learns he can rely on himself for answers.

2. Empower Your Children

Resource-parents empower their children by asking open-ended questions to guide the child to clarity about what needs to happen, such as "What do you want?" or "What's one thing you could do to solve your problem?" Rescuer-parents inadvertently minimize the resourcefulness and resilience of their children by taking over ownership of the children's problem. Teaching your children the THRIVE Principles™ will help give your children the confidence that they can take care of themselves and feel safe that they have you in their corner, cheering them on.

3. Intervene When Needed

There may be situations where it is appropriate for you to intervene in the relationship between your child and your former spouse. Any incidents involving the physical safety of your child would require action on your part, not only with your ex-spouse, but possibly also with child protection agencies or the police.

If you notice there is a persistent issue, by all means you should communicate with your ex-spouse. Decide on an appropriate means of communication. The issue itself and the urgency of it will determine whether a face-to-face meeting, phone call, or e-mail is most appropriate. Schedule a mutually convenient time to talk. Ensure you and your ex-spouse will have each other's full attention.

Start the conversation with something positive, if possible. Even a simple "Thank you for picking the kids up early last week!" can go a long way toward building goodwill. In addressing the issue, stick to the facts and describe what you've observed. Leave your personal judgment or conclusions out. If you have a specific request, make it clearly. Allow your ex-spouse time to digest and respond. If your ex-spouse gets defensive or upset, do your best to bring the discussion back to what's in the best interest of your children. Even if you don't reach an agreement in that first conversation, you've made your observations and your request. Ultimately, you'll have to decide which battles to pick.

Take Action!

1.   Write a paragraph or two about what "responsibility" means to you. Does it feel like a burden or an opportunity? What messages about responsibility did you learn growing up?

REFLECTING ON RESPONSIBILITY

To me, responsibility means:

_____

_____

_____

Take Action!

_____

_____

_____

_____

_____

_____

_____

_____

_____

_____

✔ ## Accountability Check

☐   I will complete this exercise by: _____

☐   I completed this exercise on: _____

♫ *Remember to Celebrate!* ♪

2.   It is useful to be clear about what you are and are not responsible for. Complete the following chart and then answer the question below. Feel free to add your own examples to the chart below.

Take Action!

A RESPONSIBILITY INVENTORY

Check off the appropriate column for each item.

Item	I'm responsible	I'm not responsible	I'm not sure
Your thoughts			
What your ex thinks of you			
When your child is crying			
Who your friends are			
Bedtime routines at your house			
Bedtime routines at your ex-spouse's house			
Your feelings			
What you say			
Your schedule			
Your ex not paying you child support on time			
The actions you take if your ex does not pay you child support on time			
How your ex-spouse parents your children			

Take Action!

What I noticed in completing the Responsibility Inventory was:

_____

_____

_____

_____

_____

_____

_____

_____

_____

_____

✔ Accountability Check

☐ I will complete this exercise by: _____

☐ I completed this exercise on: _____

♪ *Remember to Celebrate!* ♪

Remember to record your actions in the "Take Action!" Tracker at the end of the book.

CHAPTER TEN

Pitfall #7: Living in Chaos

"Don't judge each day by the harvest you reap,
but by the seeds you plant."

Robert Louis Stevenson

It's a big transition for children to go from living as one family with two parents under one roof to living as one family under two roofs. There's a lot of logistical and organizational planning needed to ensure the move to a "Mom's house, Dad's house" structure is smooth, while at the same time making sure that your children regain a sense of certainty and predictability in their two home environments. In a time of emotional distress, you can easily let a lot of things go, and Pitfall #7 is "Living in Chaos": rules aren't clear, schedules aren't planned, and any responsibility the child may have had for pitching in with family chores goes by the wayside in the wake of divorce.

Signs That You're Stuck

- **You don't have your children's schedule planned more than one week in advance.** Your and your former spouse have no clear agreement, understanding, or advance planning of when your children are with you and with they are with their other parent.

- **Your children consistently don't have things they need (schoolwork, clothing, sports equipment) at the house that they are in.** It's a constant struggle and source of frustration to ensure your children have what they need at the other parent's house. You end up stressed and making last-minute arrangements to get the children what they need, or they end up going without.

- **There is no consistent household routine.** Bedtimes, chores, homework expectations, and rules about electronics all vary from week to week and from house to house. Your children don't know how to load a dishwasher, set a table, make a bed, or tidy a room. Requests for help around the house are met by a chorus of "Aww, do I have to?"

- **Different rules at mom's house and dad's house cause ongoing stress and complaint.** Your children are well aware that Mom and Dad have different rules, and you find your children acting out as a result. Your children resist your standards of decorum and discipline because "they don't have to" at their other parent's house. You feel like you and your ex are being manipulated or played off each other by your children.

Your Schedule "Hot Spots"

There are predictable times in any family's life when it can get more stressful, whether you are divorced or not. I call these "hot spots" because these blocks of time often create tension or upset if you're not well prepared to handle them. Some examples include:

- getting up on time
- being ready and prepared for school
- getting homework and studying done
- mealtimes, particularly dinner
- bedtimes
- social times—having visitors into your home

For single-parent families, you can add these minefields to the "hot spot" list:

- before and after your children visit the other parent

- holidays or other special "family" occasions where one or both parents are present
- school-related events where both parents are expected to attend

Without a system in place, these "hot spot" moments can trigger chaos. Arguments break out. Anger and tension mount. Your child may start to rebel or withdraw. Sometimes the single parent, worn out from nagging and negotiating, might simply dismiss the child from being part of the solution. Other times, a bribe or promise might buy the child's cooperation in the short term, but in the long run, this solution doesn't address the chaos. The result is we enable our children to become prima donnas, excusing them from learning the life skills they'll need as responsible adults.

What's Your System?

W. Edward Demings was a world-renowned statistician and professor. He gained fame after World War II when he went to Japan and consulted with the automobile industry. His contributions revolutionized Japanese industrial quality, paving the way for Japan's enduring reputation as a preeminent technological and industrial giant.

Demings emphasized the importance of creating systems that allow an organization to reach its goals. He said that 94 percent of all breakdowns are a result of system failures, not human failures. The aim of the system must be clear to everyone in the system.

Although Demings articulated his systems theory in the context of Japanese automobile manufacturers, I believe we can apply it effectively to the single-parent household. What if 94 percent of the breakdowns we have in our family structure are because the family support system simply needs some fine-tuning? This system includes how you operate as a family unit—how you communicate with and treat each other, understanding the needs the family has to address, and understanding the role that each member has in supporting the whole family unit. Demings' theory means that only 6 percent of the time something breaks down because of the person. To get things to run smoothly, we ought to look to the system for improvement.

Have you noticed when we have a breakdown in the family, whether it's a chore left undone or an argument, we typically take that breakdown very personally? "When my kids don't pick up after themselves," shared Cindy, "I feel like they don't respect or care about me or that I've done a bad job as a mother. I can easily get upset about it. Yet when I reminded them their grandparents were coming for a visit later that day, they immediately understood and cleaned their room without complaint." In this case, Cindy's children didn't fully understand the need to be ready to greet their guests. Cindy spent her initial time and energy believing her children's behavior was a reflection on her personally, instead of making sure her children remembered the day's schedule. She could help her children remember family activities by keeping a family calendar marked with their grandparent's visit. She could have an agreement with her children that they are responsible for knowing what's on the family calendar.

Certainly our children take the system breakdowns personally. Remember how self-referential children are? It's part of how they make sense of their world. If they get into trouble or make a mistake, often their conclusion is "I'm stupid," or "I'm a bad person." It's important to teach your children that making mistakes is a great way for us all to learn. Teach your children that they have an important role to play in shaping the way your family operates.

No Structure Creates Insecurity

The need to improve our system or structure of our family is reinforced by Dr. Laurence Steinberg, a professor of psychology. In his wonderful book, *The 10 Principles of Good Parenting*, he argues that structure is the second most valuable gift we can give our children, right after the gift of love. "Some parents are reluctant to establish rules or set limits for their children because they don't want to make their children feel controlled by limits or pressured by expectations. They put themselves in their child's position and imagine what it must feel like to have other people tell you what to do all the time. And because feeling constrained by others feels bad to adults, they reason that it must feel bad to children, too," Steinberg writes. "It's a nice sentiment, but it's wrong." Based on his years of clinical practice and research, he concludes that the opposite is true: "Structure makes children feel secure."[29]

Children require structure. Having predictability and certainty about bedtimes, TV rules, mealtimes, and chores actually gives children a sense of security. With all the emotional upheaval divorce brings, your child may be comforted to know some things in his or her life can be counted on to remain the same.

"When Bob and I sat down to tell Tessa that we were going to separate, it was the most difficult moment of our lives," recalls Jane. "Bob and I had worked out together how to explain to our six-year-old that Mommy and Daddy loved her, but that we no longer loved each other, and that we were going to have to get a new home for each of us to live in. We were agonizing over how to answer the questions we thought she would ask: Why are you separating? Will you get back together? Did this mean we didn't love her? We were floored when the first question she asked was, 'Where will my toys be?'"

Jane's experience is quite typical. The children will want to know about some basic parameters that serve as the reference points for their life. Where will they live? Will they go to the same school and have the same friends? Where will the family pet live? When will I see Mommy, and when will I see Daddy? These are the kind of touchstones they need to have in place first, and from there they can process some of the more emotional issues.

The environment in which you live says a lot about you. As I learned in my training as an integrative coach, your outer world is a reflection of your inner world. There's nothing like a divorce to create turmoil in your inner emotional world. This turmoil is displayed in many external clues—missed appointments because you forgot to put them on the family calendar, dirty dishes piled in the sink, missing ingredients for a meal, stacks of unwashed or rumpled clothing spilling out of the laundry hamper or scattered on the floor. For children, this increased disorder and chaos can be very unsettling.

Logistics Are Complicated

Do you remember what it was like when you had your first child and what impact it had on your life? Suddenly new kinds of furniture, food, and routines were called for. You faced a steep learning curve as you acquired the strategic and organizational skills that being a parent requires. All parents learn these new skills, to varying degrees of success.

Having two homes with children living in each complicates the logistics of child rearing. All of a sudden, you face another learning curve. Assumptions, expectations, and rules that were the foundation of a well-run family household must now be drafted, expressed, and followed. Ideally, children should feel that they have "two homes," instead of coming from a "broken home." They should be at ease in their home with either parent.

"I had no idea how much basic information I took for granted and just carried it all around in my head," explains Marcy, the mother of ten-and twelve-year-old boys. "I want my boys to learn to be independent, so I would give them the responsibility of packing their belongings ready to go to Dad's house but they were always forgetting things. One weekend they would forget school-work, next week they would forget the soccer uniform."

Marcy needed to train her boys how to effectively pack their bags, which included knowing how long they would be away (which affected the amount of clothing they would bring), what activities they'd be doing while away (to make sure they had the soccer cleats packed), what schoolwork they had the next week, etc. "What we did together was create a checklist of things to be packed," Marcy said. "One part covered the basics they'd need every time—pajamas, toothbrush, underwear, shoes, clothing, orthodontic appliances. The next part covered special items—things they'd need for sports teams, birthday parties, any school requirements. We've got a system in place now so the boys don't feel they're reinventing the wheel each time they pack. I spend less time nagging them or driving things over to their dad's."

What's the Schedule?

Most people, young and old alike, appreciate knowing what's coming up. Last-minute schedule changes inevitably cause stress. This is more pronounced when you have children living in two different homes.

Your children need to know where they're going to be and to have advance notice. They need time to make the transition from one house to the next, and seeing it clearly marked on the refrigerator family calendar can make a world of difference. Having the schedule on the calendar provides a sense of predictability and stability at a much needed time. Even if the child-sharing schedule changes at the last minute, you can explain that to your child and show them the greater context of that change.

Be sure to spend quality time with your children. Turn the computer or Blackberry off, don't answer the phone, and give your child's after-school debriefing your full attention. If you can, build in some one-on-one time with each child so you can connect. Every child is unique, and it can be very special to connect with them solo.

Cheryl had a high-conflict divorce with the father of her two young children. It included a period where her former husband moved out of state with the children, and she had to battle through the courts to get them back. By the time she got them back, her children had experienced a lot of emotional damage and parental alienation tactics. Her daughter demanded a lot of her time and attention to deal with her various mental health and academic issues throughout her childhood. "Taking care of my daughter and her issues was so all-encompassing. My son, on the other hand, was an easy child to be with. This freed me up to put energy into her at his expense," Cheryl observed. "When he was in high school, I told him I appreciated what a great kid he was. He told me that he saw what I went through with his sister and his father. He knew I couldn't deal with anything more. I felt sad that he'd felt so much pressure on him to not give Mom more than she can deal with." Looking back on it, Cheryl realizes how important it is to give your children one-on-one time.

Don't Become a Cinderella

When you were a child, did you have certain chores to do? Standard expectations twenty to thirty years ago included things like making your bed, setting the table for dinner, feeding the dog, putting dirty clothes in the laundry hamper, sorting and folding laundry, washing the dishes after a meal, watching over a younger sibling, or raking the leaves. Go back another generation, and chores like milking the cows and mucking out the stables were on the list as well.

One impact of today's affluence in North America is that many of these chores can be delegated—to your washing machine, the gardener, the dog walker, or the housekeeper. Children today seem to be growing up with a greater sense of entitlement and diminished sense of contribution to the family's overall well-being. "I can't believe the attitude of kids these days," laments Ted, the single dad of a thirteen-year-old boy. "The other day I asked my son to set the table, and he asked me how much he would get paid! The look on my face and my stern, 'About the same amount as I do—nothing!' got him to hustle those plates onto the table."

We all know the story of Cinderella who was turned into slave labor in her own home. Don't let yourself be turned into a Cinderella parent who single-handedly maintains the household and excuses her children from playing an active part. Single parents may be more prone to catering to the whims of their children because they harbor guilt or pain about the separation. "I feel like I've asked so much of William already," fussed his mother, Marnie. "I'd love for him to be more tidy in his bedroom and the TV room, but he gets so upset when I push it. I just don't have the heart to see him in any more pain." Marnie is focused on the short-term resistance she's getting from her ten-year-old son, while overlooking the long-term benefits of encouraging her son to be responsible for the space in which he lives. William will not always have someone in his life willing to clean up his messes, and that will be a rude awakening. It is always upsetting to prima donnas when they discover they're not the only act in town.

The value of having children participate in household chores is immense. It builds their self-confidence and self-esteem and contributes to a sense of belonging within the family unit. Even the youngest child can be asked to perform a special task. The astute single parent will ensure that each child has age-appropriate chores that contribute to the family's well-being. These tasks can calm a child's fears and build a sense of stability.

Don't Forget the Discipline

Just as children need structure, they also need discipline. I'm not talking about turning your home into a finely tuned military operation, but children need guidance, guidelines, rules, and expectations. This should include relevant consequences if the rules are broken or expectations are not met.

Separated parents often struggle with discipline and exerting appropriate levels of authority because of guilt (recall Pitfall #3, Parenting from Guilt). Mom, who in the majority of cases has the lion's share of time with the children, worries that if she's too tough on the children they'll want to live with Dad. Dad fears if he's too authoritarian with his children in the limited time he has them, they may not want to come back.

If your goal is to raise healthy, responsible, trustworthy, independent, and loving adults who can work and play well with others, give your children the gift of discipline.

Creating Clarity from Chaos

You can do so many things to create clear systems in your family, and it can be overwhelming! I'm a big believer in taking simple baby steps on a consistent basis toward your goals. You are in the best position to judge where your needs are and what your priorities are. I encourage you to start with just a few simple actions to lower the chaos and increase the calm. Here are some simple ideas to get your creative juices flowing:

1. Build simple structures.
2. Create a schedule.
3. Establish communication guidelines.
4. Make acknowledgement a habit.

1. Build Simple Structures

To ensure you have clear communication, identify some of the problematic routines that challenge your peace of mind on a regular basis. After-school routines, getting prepared to spend the weekend at the other parent's house, or cleaning the kitchen properly could be examples. Here are some ideas on how to tackle them:

- Create a **process chart** so you and your children can understand what needs to happen, with whom, and by when.
- Use sticky notes to articulate the steps needed for the structure you need to create, so the problem routine you identified can run smoothly.
- After you've put each step on its own sticky note, arrange them in the order in which they should occur. Be sure to note on the paper who is responsible for each step!
- You may want to use your sticky notes to create a **checklist**. You can print off your checklist, and your child can work with it until the routine becomes a habit.
- **Charts** posted where everyone can see them are great tools for accountability for chores and responsibilities.

Making your routines more visual and creating them with your children helps to build their buy-in and participation in the solution. Don't expect them to jump with joy the first time you propose this particular family project. Children will test their limits—that's what they do, and that's how they learn. Maintain a positive attitude, and encourage your children to play a part.

If you're thinking that creating a process chart or checklist is going to "take" a lot of time, see it instead as an "investment" of your time that will save you time and energy in the long run. Figuring out simple structures for routine activities means you don't have to reinvent the wheel each time you have a visit at the other parent's house to prepare for or a chore to accomplish.

2. Create a Schedule

Strive to have clear communication with the other parent and with children about schedules. You are guaranteed to get a surly attitude and lack of cooperation if you spring something unexpected on your children at the last minute. Make sure you have a **central family calendar** that clearly marks when the children are with each parent. All major school, family, sporting, and community commitments should also be noted. Encourage your children to refer to the calendar so they can plan ahead. When your children are old enough, they can add to the family calendar on their own initiative.

Some single parents find it helpful for each child to have a **log book** or communication journal. The book stays with the child and is used by both parents to note the child's mood and health status, share reminders about upcoming events, and share special accomplishments. This way, both parents get a more complete picture of their child's day and can easily share valuable information.

Some interesting online tools are available that allow you to share information about your child with the other parent. There are a number of products out there now that offer features such as a secure database that can house not only all the data about your child (including teachers, medical history, etc.), but also an electronic calendar color coded for each child and tools to track child-related expenses.

3. Establish Communications Guidelines

Many parents, whether divorced or married, often make the mistake of endlessly reminding and nagging children when it comes to their responsibilities. Have you noticed how children can sometimes appear to be deaf to their parents? Yet, how many times do you have to ask them if they want a chocolate chip cookie? Clearly children's hearing (and adult's too) can be selective. It's important to follow up words with actions.

Make sure your **expectations** for your children about family chores, schoolwork, and manners are clear. Identifying your steps and routines with them will help with this. If you run into problems, avoid jumping into instant-dictator mode, and instead involve your children in some joint problem solving and brainstorming. This demonstrates that you value and respect them. Holding **family meetings** on a regular basis is a great way to build a sense of teamwork, do some planning, and solve problems together.

If the mood is getting heated, agree to take a break. You're not going to make much headway if a temper tantrum is brewing. Simply acknowledge you can see tempers are starting to flare and that you will reschedule the conversation later. Need to break the tension? Try putting on some loud music and start a dance demonstration. Have a tickle fight or a family cuddle. Remember to keep your vision in mind, and know you will move through the day-to-day challenges that can come up.

If you are coparenting your child with your ex, it's important you have some agreements as to how you're going to communicate. We've already talked about treating your ex-partner more like a business partner than a former lover. If you agree to e-mail each other, what length of time can you agree to wait before a response must be sent? Should you have a regular weekly or monthly check-in conversation, either in phone or in person? What about an annual planning session to figure out summer holiday plans or after-school activities? The better and clearer your communication with each other is, the more clarity and peace of mind you'll enjoy.

Your children's schedule should be included specifically in your parenting plan as part of your separation agreement. Be sure to establish a protocol for what happens if one parent is unable to be with the children on the day that the parent is supposed to spend. Who is responsible for finding alternate child care? If you make a change in the children's schedule, do you need to make a compensating trade of time with the children? If so, in what timeframe—that same month? That quarter? In creating your parenting plan, take the time to anticipate and work out the details to these kinds of issues so you have a common understanding of how this is to work.[30]

4. Make a Habit of Acknowledgment

The most important step here is to continually acknowledge and appreciate the progress you as a family are making as you bring yourselves out of chaos and into greater clarity. It's a team effort, and every player has a job to do. Take the time to acknowledge your team members and make that a life-long habit.

Relationship experts estimate that it takes five appreciations to counterbalance the negative impact of even one criticism. Research also shows that acts of kindness, such as appreciation, can alter the brain chemistry in a positive way, elevating our mood and sense of well-being. This change is enjoyed not only by the recipient of the act of kindness, but also by the giver and even third-party witnesses to the act. One simple act of appreciation provides a big payoff to many people!

Take the time to acknowledge your children's efforts. Thank them for their questions. Thank your ex for bringing the children back to you on time. Don't forget to appreciate yourself as well! Appreciation and acknowledgment are the lubrication that will help ensure the operations of your family system run smoothly.

Take Action!

1. Pick one idea from this chapter that you are prepared to do to create greater clarity and structure in your family. It could be to start a family calendar or sit down with your children to discuss how to pack their bags and be ready to go to their other parent's house. Implement this idea within seven days.

Take Action!

MY ACTION STEP

Within the next seven days, I will:

_____

_____

_____

_____

_____

_____

_____

_____

✔ ## Accountability Check

☐   I will complete this exercise by: _____

☐   I completed this exercise on: _____

♫ *Remember to Celebrate!*

Take Action!

2.   Map out a typical week in your family as it is right now. Notice how much downtime there is. Identify a block of time you can spend together as a family. See where you can schedule one-on-one time with each of your children. If this is impossible to do with your current schedule, what would you be willing to give up if having more quality time together is a priority for you? Identify one tangible step you can take to have more one-on-one time with your children. If you only have one child, identify one thing you could do to make some special time together. Share the results with your children and discuss it together.

ONE-ON-ONE TIME

I can create more one-on-one time to connect with my child(ren) by:

_____

_____

_____

_____

_____

_____

_____

_____

Take Action!

 ## Accountability Check

☐   I will complete this exercise by: _____

☐   I completed this exercise on: _____

♫ *Remember to Celebrate!* 🎤

Remember to record your actions in the "Take Action!" Tracker at the end of the book.

PART FOUR

THRIVE AFTER DIVORCE

CHAPTER ELEVEN

Forging the Path Ahead

"Do not go where the path may lead, go instead where there is no path and leave a trail."

Ralph Waldo Emerson

Many would agree that parenting and divorce are two of life's biggest challenges. Many people would agree that being a parent is also one of life's biggest rewards and blessings. We learn so much about ourselves and what we are made of when we take on the responsibility to love and raise another human being.

I wonder how many people would join me in saying that getting divorced can also be one of life's biggest rewards and blessings. Please don't think that I'm an advocate for divorce and that more people should run out and get one. Not at all. What I am saying is if an intimate relationship is unhappy, unfulfilling, or even unsafe, divorce may be what's needed.

Rather than viewing divorce as a shameful admission of failure, I would encourage you to shift your perspective to one of curiosity and wonder. Ask yourself if you're willing to wring every drop of wisdom and life lessons for yourself from your divorce experience? Are you willing to allow your divorce to open up a new kind of relationship with your children that's founded on conscious choice and partnership? Are you ready to take the bull by the horns and thrive after divorce? If you've read this far in the book, I'll venture to say your answer to these questions is yes, and I acknowledge you for your commitment.

Thrive after Divorce—Do It for Your Children

My children gave me the fuel I needed to heal from my divorce. Going through my divorce, I was definitely hurting and confused. Seeing the hurt and confusion in my children's faces as I interacted with them in those early days woke me up and motivated me to do whatever it took to heal my heart so I could love them fully. I could see that if I shrank back from making tough decisions or denied my pain, I would pass on a heritage of denial and martyrdom to my children. I didn't want to leave that legacy. I would rather my children grow up with their own unique struggles and dramas and learn to solve them, rather than recycling or repeating their mother's emotional issues!

Children are the innocent victims of divorce. Whether it's through the divorce process itself or the cold war between ex-spouses that can ensue afterward, children pay the price. They pay the price in their self-esteem and their ability to create successful intimate relationships of their own. Some children act out their pain through lower academic achievement, falling in with the wrong peer group, using drugs, committing crimes, and more.

What kind of legacy do you want to leave your children now that you are divorced? The impact of how you raise your children goes even beyond your immediate family. Think of the ripples created when you drop a stone into a pond. The immediate circle is your biological family. Your children in turn have an impact on their friends and peer group. The ripples, in turn, affect the broader community and society in which we live.

Do you realize how you raise your children has a huge impact that extends far beyond the current generation? What choices would you make in how you parent your children if you consider you are raising the parent of your grand-children or the great-grandparent of your great-great-grandchildren?

Thrive after Divorce—Do It for Yourself

Ultimately, the most important relationship you need to cultivate and heal is the one you have with yourself. Your relationship with yourself determines the quality of relationship you can have with anyone else. It profoundly affects the quality of the relationship you can have with your children as well.

Among my friends, I had the reputation of being a very compassionate person. People could count on me to listen and support them in any way I could. The divorce forced me to turn my lens onto myself. I was amazed at how little compassion, listening, and trust I had for myself. My divorce revealed to me how little responsibility I had assumed for my own well-being and happiness. I had been blindly putting the burden of my happiness and self-worth into the hands of other people—my children, my husband, my friends, and my work colleagues. One of the greatest gifts from my divorce has been to learn how to trust myself and to realize the only person who needed to approve of me was me!

Ultimately, we are the co-creators of our reality. You deserve to thrive and flourish after divorce. This book has given you several tools and insights to help you and your children. In closing, I offer these affirmations based on the THRIVE Principles™. If you'd like to receive a free electronic copy of them for you to post up as reminders, please visit www.7pitfalls.com.

TRUST

- I trust myself. I trust that everything happens for a reason. I trust that I can handle everything life brings me.

HONESTY

- I am willing to tell the truth to myself and others. Honesty really is the best policy.

RESPONSIBILITY

- I am responsible for my thoughts, words, and actions. I am responsible for my own self-care.

INTEGRITY

- I do what I say. I say what I do. I am a person of my word.

VISION

- I am fueled and guided by the big picture I create for my life. I am willing to move toward my vision, even if I don't know "how" I will get there.

EXPRESSION

- I am committed to being my authentic self. I express all my emotions in healthy ways. I feel vital and alive.

Let's Make a Deal

If you've come this far in the book, you are clearly motivated to make a change. Let's make a deal, shall we? Try some of the action steps. Simply allow yourself to experiment with them. You can try on the THRIVE Principles™ and affirmations for a week.

If you don't notice a change in your mind-set or a feeling of lightness opening up inside your heart, you have a choice to make. You can continue on anyway, fueled by your vision. Or, you can always go back to your old ways. You may not be willing to give up some of these pitfalls right away. Progress is more important than perfection. The point is to become aware of these pitfalls and choose a different strategy that can better support you and your children.

The important thing is to simply start somewhere and take action. Get started today! I have no doubt you will see some great things starting to open up as a result.

ENDNOTES

1   Fadi Baradihi and Nancy Kurn, The IDFA Divorce Survival Guide (Michigan: IDFA Publishing, 2006).

2   Constance Ahrons, *The Good Divorce: Keeping Your Family Together When Your Marriage Comes Apart* (New York: HarperCollins Publisher, 1994), p 31. Ahrons explains there is a wide range of estimated divorce rates. Factors influencing the divorce rate include the aging of the baby boomers, increasing financial independence of women, and higher life expectancy rates.

3   U.S. Census Bureau and Statistics Canada data from 1997, as cited by www.divorcemag.com.

4   Shellee Darnell, MFT, "How to Be The Best Single Parent You Can," www.divorcewizards.com.

5   Fadi Baradihi and Nancy Kurn. The IDFA Divorce Survival Guide (Michigan: IDFA Publishing, 2006).

6   Presentation by Dr. Joan B. Kelly, PhD, on "Divorce and Children's Adjustment: Current Research and Implications for Practice," Toronto, ON on April 26, 2007. Dr. Kelly and Judith S. Wallerstein authored *Surviving the Breakup* (New York, Basic Books, reprinted 1996), which has been called the book that revolutionized America's thinking about children and divorce.

7   Ibid., p 126-127.

8   Dr. Bruce Fisher and Dr. Robert Alberti, *Rebuilding When Your Relationship Ends* 3rd ed (Atascadero, California: Impact Publishers, Inc., 2001), p 6.

9   See for example Ibid or Elisabeth Kubler-Ross, *On Death and Dying* (Riverside, NJ, Scribner, 1997), which articulated five stages of death (denial, anger, bargaining, depression, and acceptance).

10   Many of these principles have been part of my personal mission since I was a young girl, but I would like to gratefully acknowledge some of the authors I've studied and my own personal teachers who have helped me to live these principles more fully in my own life. In particular I would like to acknowledge the writings of Wayne Dyer, and my trainings with Debbie Ford, Kathlyn Hendricks, T. Harv Eker and Landmark Education.

11   Stephen M. R. Covey, *The Speed of Trust: The One Thing That Changes Everything* (New York: Free Press, 2006), p 46.

12   One of the best books on the subject of making conscious choices is Debbie Ford's *The Right Questions: Ten Essential Questions to Guide You to an Extraordinary Life* (HarperCollins, 2003). She offers ten simple yet powerful questions you can ask yourself in any moment of choice to guide you in the direction of your goals.

13   Michael J. Losier, *Law of Attraction: The Science of Attracting More of What You Want and Less of What You Don't* (Vancouver, BC: Michael J. Losier Enterprises Inc., 2006), p 9.

14   Personal interview with Debbie Ford.

15   Personal interview with Vered Neta.

16   Don Miguel Ruiz, *The Four Agreements* (San Rafael, CA: Amber-Allen Publishing, 1997).

17   Ibid., p 12.

18   Personal interview with Debbie Ford.

19   Personal interview with Michael Cochrane.

20   To learn more, do a Web search of the term "collaborative law" in your state or province, and you'll find links to lawyers using this method. A good reference book that provides an overview of how the collaborative divorce process works is *The Collaborative Way to Divorce: The Revolutionary Method That Results in Less Stress, Lower Costs, and Happier Kids–Without Going to Court* (New York: Hudson Street Press, 2006) by Stuart G. Webb and Ronald D. Ousky.

21   Personal interview with Debbie Ford.

22   Personal interview with Wouter van der Hall.

23   Laurence Steinberg, *The 10 Basic Principles of Good Parenting* (New York: Simon & Schuster Paperbacks, 2004), p 27–28.

24   Ibid, p 29.

25   Rahe Miller, *Social Readjustment Rating Scale* (1997) as cited in Hanna McDonough & Christina Bartha, *Putting Children First: A Guide For Parents Breaking Up* (Toronto: University of Toronto Press, 2000), p.12–14.

26   Presentation by Dr. Joan Kelly on "Divorce and Children's Adjustment: Current Research and Implications for Practice," Toronto, ON, April 26, 2007.

27   Richard A. Warshak, *Divorce Poison: Protecting the Parent-Child Bond from a Vindictive Ex* (New York: HarperCollins Publishers, 2003), p 16–17.

28   Interview with Michael Cochrane.

29   Laurence Steinberg, *The 10 Basic Principles of Good Parenting* (New York: Simon & Schuster Paperbacks, 2004), p 87–88.

30   Isolina Ricci's *Mom's House, Dad's House: Making Two Homes For Your Child* (New York: Fireside, 1997) and Hanna McDonough and Christina Bartha's *Putting Children First: A Guide for Parents Breaking Up* (Toronto: University of Toronto Press, 2000) offer great strategies and recommendations for creating an effective parenting plan.

YOUR "TAKE ACTION!" TRACKER

Chapter Two—Where Are You Right Now?

Take Action! Item	Date Completed
Take the 7 Pitfalls of Single Parenting Self-Assessment quiz. To take the online version, visit visit www.7pitfalls.com.	
Retake the self-assessment survey ninety days later.	

Chapter Three—The THRIVE Principles™

Take Action! Item	Date Completed
Write out the THRIVE Principles™ and post them where you'll see them.	
Create your personal affirmation for each THRIVE Principle. You can visit www.7pitfalls.com to download a blank template to complete this exercise.	

Chapter Four—Pitfall #1: Not Having a Big Picture

Take Action! Item	Date Completed
1. Take thirty minutes to reflect on what vision means to you.	
2. Write a one-page description of your inspiring new vision.	

Chapter Five—Pitfall #2: Getting Hooked by Your Ex-spouse

Take Action! Item	Date Completed
1. Complete "My 'Martyr Medal' Events" exercise.	
2. Complete the "Advance Planning Guide" exercise.	

Chapter Six—Pitfall #3: Parenting from Guilt

Take Action! Item	Date Completed
1. Complete the "Building My Awareness of Guilt" exercise.	
2. Complete "Lessons I Can Learn from My Divorce" exercise.	
3. Complete "Lessons My Children Can Learn from My Divorce" exercise.	

Chapter Seven—Pitfall #4: Going for the Martyr Medal

Take Action! Item	Date Completed
1. Complete "My Martyr Medal Events" exercise.	
2. Write your prescription for the "I wanna be a martyr" syndrome. To download a worksheet for this exercise, you can visit www.7pitfalls.com	
3. Play the Appreciation Game.	

Chapter Eight—Pitfall #5: Not Putting Your Children First

Take Action! Item	Date Completed
1. Complete the "Eyes on the Prize" exercise.	
2. Complete the "Defining My Children's Best Interests" exercise.	

Chapter Nine—Pitfall #6: Being Responsible for Your Children's Relationship with Your Ex

Take Action! Item	Date Completed
1. Complete "Reflecting on Responsibility" exercise.	
2. Complete the "Responsibility Inventory" exercise.	

Chapter Ten—Pitfall #7: Living in Chaos

Take Action! Item	Date Completed
1. Identify one idea to implement to bring clarity from chaos.	
2. Map out a typical week and assess it for quality time. Complete the "One-on-One Time" exercise.	

CELEBRATE YOUR ACCOMPLISHMENTS!

RECOMMENDED RESOURCES

Ahrons, Constance. *The Good Divorce: Keeping Your Family Together When Your Marriage Comes Apart*. New York: HarperCollins Publishing, 1994.

Ahrons, Constance. *We're Still Family: What Grown Children Have to Say About Their Parents' Divorce*. New York: HarperCollins Publishing, 2004.

Baradihi, Fadi and Nancy Kurn. *The IDFA Divorce Survival Guide*. Michigan MI: IDFA Publishing, 2006.

Cochrane, Michael G. *Surviving Your Divorce: A Guide to Canadian Family Law*. 4th ed. Toronto: Wiley Press, 2007.

Cochrane, Michael G. *Surviving Your Parents' Divorce: A Guide for Young Canadians*. 2nd ed. Toronto: Wiley Press, 1999.

Covey, Stephen M. R. and Rebecca R. Merrill. *The Speed of Trust: The One Thing That Changes Everything*. New York: Free Press, 2006.

Covey, Stephen R. *The 7 Habits of Highly Effective Families*. New York: Golden Books, 1997.

De Angelis, Barbara. *How Did I Get Here? Finding Your Way to Renewed Hope and Happiness When Life and Love Take Unexpected Turns*. New York: St. Martin's Press, 2005.

Dyer, Wayne W. *The Power of Intention: Learning to Co-create Your World Your Way*. Carlsbad, CA: Hay House, 2004.

Eker, T. Harv. *Secrets of the Millionaire Mind: Mastering the Inner Game of Wealth*. Toronto: HarperCollins Publishers, 2005.

Emery, Robert E. *The Truth About Children and Divorce*. Toronto: Penguin Group, 2006.

Fisher, Bruce and Robert Alberti. *Rebuilding When Your Relationship Ends*. 3rd ed. Atascadero, California: Impact Publishers, Inc., 2001.

Ford, Debbie. *The Best Year of Your Life: Dream It, Plan It, Live It*. New York: HarperCollins, 2005.

Ford, Debbie. *The Dark Side of the Light Chasers: Reclaiming Your Power, Creativity, Brilliance and Dreams*. New York: Riverhead Books, 1998.

Ford, Debbie. *The Right Questions: Ten Essential Questions to Guide You to an Extraordinary Life*. New York: HarperCollins, 2003.

Ford, Debbie. *The Secret of the Shadow: The Power of Owning Your Whole Story*. New York: HarperCollins, 2002.

Ford, Debbie. *Spiritual Divorce: Divorce as a Catalyst for An Extraordinary Life*. New York: HarperCollins, 2001. For information on teleclasses and workshops, visit www.debbieford.com.

Friel, John C. and Linda D. Friel. *The 7 Worst Things Parents Do*. Deerfield Beach, FL: Health Communications Inc., 1999.

Jeffers, Susan. *Feel the Fear and Do It Anyway*. New York: Random House, 1987.

Hendricks, Gay, and Kathlyn Hendricks, PhD. *Lasting Love: The 5 Secrets of Growing a Vital Conscious Relationship*. New York: Rodale, 2004.

Hetherington, E. Mavis and John Kelly. *For Better or For Worse: Divorce Reconsidered*. New York: W.W. Norton & Company Ltd., 2002.

Hicks, Esther and Jerry Hicks. *Ask and It Is Given: Learning to Manifest Your Desires*. Carlsbad, CA: Hay House Inc., 2004.

Lintermans, Gloria. *The Newly Divorced Book of Protocol: How to Be Civil When You Hate Their Guts*. New York: Barricade Books Inc., 1995.

Losier, Michael J. *Law of Attraction: The Science of Attracting More of What You Want and Less of What You Don't.* Victoria, BC: Michael J. Losier Enterprises Inc., 2006.

Maltz, Maxwell. *The New Psycho-Cybernetics.* New York: Penguin Putnam, 2001.

McDonough, Hanna and Christina Bartha. *Putting Children First: A Guide for Parents Breaking Up.* Toronto: University of Toronto Press, 2000.

Neta, Nisandeh and Vered Neta, *The Art of Lovemaking: Couples' Guide to a Passionate Sex Life.* Charleston, SC: BookSurge Publishing, 2005. See also www.no-problem-marriage-counseling.com.

Ricci, Isolina. *Mom's House, Dad's House: Making Two Homes For Your Child.* New York: Fireside, 1997.

Ross, Julie A. and Judy Corcoran. *Joint Custody with a Jerk: Raising a Child with an Uncooperative Ex.* New York: St. Martin's Press, 1996.

Ruiz, Don Miguel. *The Four Agreements.* San Rafael, CA: Amber-Allen Publishing, 1997.

Steinberg, Laurence. *The 10 Basic Principles of Good Parenting.* New York: Simon and Schuster, 2004.

Tolle, Eckhardt. *A New Earth: Awakening to Your Life's Purpose.* New York: Penguin Group, 2005.

Tolle, Eckhardt. *The Power of Now: A Guide to Spiritual Enlightenment.* Vancouver: Namaste Publishing, 1997.

Vitale, Joe. *The Attractor Factor: 5 Easy Steps for Creating Wealth (or Anything Else) From the Inside Out.* Hoboken, NJ: John Wiley & Sons, 2005.

Wallerstein, Judith S. and Sandra Blakeslee. *What About the Kids? Raising Your Children Before, During, and After Divorce.* New York: Hyperion, 2003.

Wallerstein, Judith S. and Joan B Kelly. *Surviving the Breakup.* New York: Basic Books, 1996 (reprinted).

Warshak, Dr. Richard A. *Divorce Poison: Protecting the Parent-Child Bond from a Vindictive Ex*. New York: HarperCollins Publishers Inc., 2003.

Webb, Stuart G. and Ronald D. Ousky. *The Collaborative Way to Divorce: The Revolutionary Method That Results in Less Stress, Lower Costs, and Happier Kids—Without Going to Court*. New York: Hudson Street Press, 2006.

Wittman, Jeffrey P. *Custody Chaos, Personal Peace: Sharing Custody with an Ex Who Drives You Crazy*. New York: Penguin Publishing, 2001.

7 PITFALLS OF SINGLE PARENTING RESOURCES

There are a number of resources available for you to support you with the material contained in *The 7 Pitfalls of Single Parenting: What to Avoid to Help Your Children Thrive After Divorce.*

Visit www.7pitfalls.com to get:

Chapter Three	Online "7 Pitfalls of Single Parenting Self-Assessment Quiz"
Chapter Four	Worksheet–Blank template for THRIVE Principles™ Affirmations
Chapter Eight	Worksheet–Your Prescription for the "I wanna be a martyr" syndrome

THRIVE Principles™ Affirmations

You can also purchase a copy of *The 7 Pitfalls of Single Parenting Workbook* by visiting www.7pitfalls.com. This workbook offers more in-depth exercises, and questions to help you understand and integrate the information you've learned.

I WOULD LOVE TO HEAR
HOW YOU ARE DOING!

Congratulate yourself for completing this book and taking an important step in your divorce journey! Thank you for choosing to thrive after divorce! You and your children most certainly deserve to thrive and flourish. It is my deepest wish that this book has opened some new possibilities for you and for family to do just that!

I would love to hear how you are doing! Would you like to share your experience in working with the THRIVE Principles™ and overcoming the 7 pitfalls of single parenting? I hope you can agree that we learn so much from hearing other people's stories. I would love to hear what you've learned and how your life has changed. If you'd like to offer a testimonial of your experience, I could share what you've learned in one of my future books or on my website.

I've created a 7 Pitfalls feedback form so you can do just that. Please visit www.7pitfalls.com/feedback.

Thank you for your feedback!

THRIVE AFTER DIVORCE

From my own personal experience with divorce, I was inspired to see how making the choice to thrive after divorce could turn my life around in a positive and all-encompassing way. I realized that my personal mission is to empower people to fearlessly create and express their highest potential. You can learn more about the success strategies and resources I have created for seperated and divorced individuals by visiting www.ThriveAfterDivorce.com.

Reading this book and doing the exercises is a great first step. I'd like to invite you to take advantage of some of the other resources Thrive after Divorce has to offer you.

The Thrive Guide e-zine

This FREE bi-weekly electronic newsletter, or e-zine, offers tips, strategies, and resources for separated and divorced individuals. It includes an "Ask Thrive after Divorce" column that answers questions submitted by the readers. To sub-scribe, visit www.ThriveAfterDivorce.com

The Divorce Resource Kit

The award-winning Divorce Resource Kit helps you put all the pieces of your divorce puzzle back together again - quickly, effectively, clearly, just the way YOU want them to fit. From dating to parenting, finances to legal options, or just getting your emotional balance back after divorce, this is your personalized road map for how you and your family can thrive after divorce.

Includes audio interviews, checklists, exercises, suggested scripts and more. Within 15 minutes you can get absolute clarity on your plan of action for each piece of your divorce puzzle. The Divorce Resource Kit will save you time, money, and heartache!

The Divorce Resource Kit received the Apex Award for Publication Excellence. Also available in a Downloadable Edition, so you can have it delivered to your email in-box within minutes!

For more information, visit www.DivorceResourceKit.com

Ask Thrive after Divorce

Is there a question or issue you're facing that you'd like support with? Please visit www.thriveafterdivorce.com/ask.html, and submit your question. We'll do our very best to answer your question in upcoming issues of the Thrive Guide e-zine.

ABOUT THE AUTHOR

Carolyn B. Ellis is a Success Strategist, award-winning author, and the Founder of ThriveAfterDivorce.com and BrillianceMastery.com. A Harvard University graduate, she has trained with some of the world's greatest transformational and marketing leaders. She has in fact been engaged by many of them to assist their personal clients with their business and coaching needs.

Carolyn is a Certified Master Integrative Coach™, Voice Dialogue facilitator and was the first Canadian to be certified as a Spiritual Divorce Coach by Debbie Ford's Institute for Integrative Coaching. She is also a Certified Money, Marketing and Soul Coach ™ and a Money Breakthrough Method ™ Coach. She currently serves as Co-Director of Advanced Programs for Shakti Communications and the work of world-renowned transformational teacher and *New York Times* best-selling author, Dr. Barbara De Angelis.

Carolyn has created a number of award-winning educational resources for divorced women and men. These include the *Divorce Resource Kit, The 7 Pitfalls of Single Parenting: What to Avoid to Help Your Children Thrive after Divorce* and *Parenting after Divorce 101*. Her publications have a proven track record of helping those experiencing divorce turn adversity into opportunity and pave the way for a life of passion, vitality and success.

In 2009, Carolyn founded www.BrillianceMastery.com to help brilliant women and conscious entrepreneurs reconstruct and realign their businesses in order to present their great work more clearly, powerfully and profitably to the world. She publishes the "Bits of Brilliance" and THRIVE Guide e-newsletters, which are enjoyed by thousands of subscribers from across the globe.

Carolyn's easy-to-understand and holistic advice has been featured regularly in *The Globe and Mail, MacLean's Magazine, Divorce Magazine*, CITY-TV, CBC radio and TV, as she passionately works to bring forth strategies of personal, business and financial mastery to women all across the globe.

She lives in Toronto, ON and enjoys musical theatre, meditation, and yoga.

Her three amazing children and bouncy labradoodle dog are her daily sources of inspiration and joy.

For more information about separation and divorce, please visit www.ThriveAfterDivorce.com.

For more information about creating a successful business based on your life's purpose, please visit www.BrillianceMastery.com.